Getting onto the Bridge of Actualising Self-full Love

The Crimson Light Volume 2

CRIMEY QUEEN

authorHOUSE®

AuthorHouse™ UK
1663 Liberty Drive
Bloomington, IN 47403   USA
www.authorhouse.co.uk
Phone: 0800.197.4150

Scripture quotations marked KJV are from the Holy Bible, King James Version (Authorized Version). First published in 1611. Quoted from the KJV Classic Reference Bible, Copyright © *1983 by The Zondervan Corporation.*

Published by AuthorHouse 06/01/2016

ISBN: 978-1-5246-2847-5 (sc)
ISBN: 978-1-5246-2845-1 (hc)
ISBN: 978-1-5246-2846-8 (e)

Print information available on the last page.

Any people depicted in stock imagery provided by Thinkstock are models, and such images are being used for illustrative purposes only. Certain stock imagery © *Thinkstock.*

This book is printed on acid-free paper.

Once, a time, at the core of every man and woman
Reigned the spirit of the Crimson Light
It was believed all things were possible
And that all of life's answers, are played out
In everyday scenarios; and especially,
When we lay our heads down to sleep
Of which, we call dreams and visions
That sadly, many simply dismiss,
The guidance, to follow the cues;
Of their internal Global Programming System.

Without any recollection of where you've been
Or who you met, and what you did in the night;
Like when you take an aeroplane flight;
Do, you pay attention to the person next to you?
As you say, or may even hear,
"Excuse me, I need to go to the washroom"
Never-mind, that names were not exchanged
Perhaps something more profound had been engaged
Which confirms, there is always 'hope for the people.'

Somewhere, deep in your brain
You have been left with the lasting memory
That you have been touched
Either by a sinner or a saint;
Nevertheless, I employ you,
This is never to drive you insane
Only to encourage you to let go of your extra load,
And to pay attention to the signs
That present themselves in dream and vision
To make light your 'final destination resort.'

Contents

Acknowledgements...ix

Introduction...xi

Why Be Afraid? 1

A Mother's Consent to the Light 18

Signpost to the Bridge..51

Your Boarding Pass to the Bridge...76

Bridge Construction...98

It's a Love Thing...127

Why Are You Here?...151

I Know Why I am Here 166

ACKNOWLEDGEMENTS

The Crimson Light is expressed through all the elders: Faith, Unity, Truth, Presence, Forgiveness, Conviction, and Endurance.

The wondrous gifts of the spirit of Wisdom, Healing, Knowledge, Prophesy, Language and Faith, Miracles, and Discernment which works as one spirit and is available to to all people on the earth.

For those who are seeking their passion through the gifts of the spirit: May the Crimson Light guide you.

For all mothers and mothers of mothers, who are yet to find your voices, including others who have offered their voices so that the daughters of the world can also find the courage to speak and honour their truth.

For all fathers, and fathers of fathers who are hurting and have not learned how to constructively deal with your pain: Remember, your gain lies in your legacy as the sons and daughters through whom your light shines on the earth.

For my loving son Daniel including all the sons who have not found their strength by learning how to cry. Remember, there is healing in the tears.

Nieces and nephews with absent parents, may you find your inner strength and purpose to pave the way for the new generation.

Alex Amponsah for your continued loyalty and support.

For my siblings, family, and friends, who have all enriched my life: May the Crimson Light continue to shine on all. Thank you.

For everyone and every creature, place, and institution that has touched my life directly and indirectly, through all of which I have now gained my sense of wholeness in discovering the spirit of Lauviah.

INTRODUCTION

What greater love has a man than to literally step into a tombed casket, just like that?

After I had witnesssed Mr. Barack Altidore stepping into the tomb casket just like that, I had to revisit the road once travelled on the tropical island of St Lucia so that I could move forward.

The decision to forge ahead with determination and to leave no stone unturned had made me examine the ties that bind the emotional fabric of my family. A colourful fabric, but one only made visible after being dusted and displayed its various facets through the paradox of my beliefs and experiences. I had been faced with the aftermath of the marriage of my attention and intention involved, to ease the jagged graphs of my emotions, the feelings of failure, and accept the elation of my achievements and to validate my need for a four word question: why are you here?

Basically, I had not understood the brightness of the hills and the blackness of smoky valleys that had shaped my life, as Lauviah.

I had seen for myself that the allegiance of the Crimson Light had not failed me. Although birthed through pain of feeling rejected, it permitted me to see that love is often nearer than breath.

That, in turn, was how I collected not one but seven trophies that formed the combination of Actualising Self-full Love.

Now all this had happened as a result of the choice I had made to be escorted into the basement of Grazebrook Primary School (GPS). It was in the school yard that I was escorted by a woman in black, Mrs Blanchard's look-alike, in search of my diary. Afterwards, I discovered, I had woken up in the middle of the night to a series of strange events. Along with a bunch of keys in my hand, there were the brightest crimson lights I had ever seen. This, however, was not excluding my ability to communicate with a six-inch-thick wall and two dogs.

I had made a jump in time, and to my surprise, outside GPS, it was like broad daylight. Unlike the wall and the dogs, I seemed unable to communicate with the three men I saw standing outside, who totally disregarded anything I had to say.

I believe that the resonance of the light that had hovered over me, as I gazed at the beautiful cornfield that surrounded the buildings, made me realise the sacredness of what was to take place. And now I am ready to commence the second part of my journey and to further explore my relationship with the Crimson light that so far, has dealt me no half measures in igniting my will and spirit; which tends to spiral my journey into a series of unexpected junctures. Although this meant I had to rely on my intuition to explore the various subjects that seemed to bear more thorns than petals in my body mind and spirit.

It might have been that the director of this grand universe had convinced me that nothing happens by chance but by the choices that we make. Based on that premise, I held the belief that I had been there along with Harry and Christian as witnesses to Mr Barack Altidore, the owner of the Hope for the People (HFTP) infirmary and the Final Destination Resort mortuary (FDR), descending into what I could only describe as a tombed casket, just like that.

Unbeknownst at the time, the decision to seek my missing diary from Grazebrook Primary School, which my son attended, was necessary since it birthed the role by which I would act out for my secret passion of being a movie star. Just so that I could not only prove to myself but proclaim to the world my true identity, yet my training, so far, had not been without the influence of inherent friends and who also happened to be devoted members of the cast.

It would seem, as a result of my desire, the dancing rays of the Crimson Light not only fuelled my desire to Actualise Self-full Love but remained committed to guiding me, and now I am presented the module Why Be Afraid?

Therefore, my intention for you as my companion is to make this journey one of personal transformation, as I venture once more under the constant illumination and guidance of the Crimson Light that is always alive in everything and in every dream. As I endeavour to find my identity, let's make this a glorious trip to the Bridge of Actualising Self-full Love.

Chapter 1

Why Be Afraid?

Fear makes us afraid and even petrified of ourselves, but there's no denying that Fear, like my loyal friends Chatterbox and Resignation, has been good to me. Fear alerts me to many dangers, even in my failure to foresee what is potentially detrimental or even fatal. So why be afraid? Conversely, I have experienced being with Fear, and with the frightening feeling that my intestines had been ruptured and that my heart was an atomic bomb just waiting to explode. As a result, my relationship with Fear often seems a muddled one. Hence, there is an awareness that Fear operates from subtle to drastic measures and, therefore, appears to be eternally with me. However, my occupation at present is to seek an understanding of Fear, so that I may fine-tune my internal make-up for getting onto the Bridge of Actualising Self-full Love. As a result, I am now continuing to trust the constant guidance and illumination of the Crimson Light and to see how Fear operate in our lives.

It would seem like we generally disguise our frightful thoughts and feelings, so that Fear is no longer for us the guy with bulging eyes and two horns. Instead, like the Hollywood actor Tom Hanks, in the movie Castaway, we tend to mollify Fear, make the face value of our transformed condition the new reality.

As the only survivor of a FedEx plane crash, Hanks discovers that he is the only human being on a deserted tropical island; ultimately, he is forced to face his deepest fears. He not only has to contend with staying alive but is also consumed with a burning desire to reunite with the people and places that really matter to him. Through a battle of wits, Hanks resorts to drawing a face on a volleyball named Wilson. During their four years on the island, Hanks shared his fears and other feelings with the ball.

The golden opportunity arrived, and Hanks ensured to take his companion with him to begin a journey into the unknown, one of faith, to be rescued from the island. However, circumstances would determine otherwise, as Hanks had failed to reach Wilson, who had gotten carried away by the tide. As the two drifted farther apart from each other, one could conclude they had reached the climax of their covert agreement. As a sense of this acceptance, having fulfilled his purpose, Wilson deliberately allowed himself to drift away. Whilst Hanks, on the other hand, seemed to desperately wish it were not so and was forced to accept the fact that he had to let go. He just had to let go to allow himself the chance to be rescued without his friend. And this leaves me wondering, Why do we always feel the need to engage in a game with Fear?

Perhaps it is also safe to conclude that even when we say that we are having a ball, in essence, because we are afraid, we put on a face that we believe will grant the outcome that we want. In short, we manipulate Fear, so that we can tolerate him. You could say, the game with Wilson is a way of pacifying the godfather of anger, power, and control. In which case, our behaviour towards Wilson can be viewed as the game of guardian and child. But the problem arises only when we are unsure of who is in control.

For instance, we learn to hide, like an unhappy child with a lovely painted butterfly on his face, by which we can shift the focus of attention from which to hide. Progressively, the child identifies with us, by reciprocating a matching expression on his face. He proceeds to play whatever games we want to act out. In addition, we become very creative by convincing him that what is apparent is not only true, but it is all actually his idea, and that he is in total control, and then we baptise Wilson.

When things don't work out the way we want them to, we convince ourselves that our unhappiness is really Wilson's fault. This may be due to Wilson's roundness and adaptability and readiness to just roll into any sporting position of our intention. Adding to this, we often deny the pain that serves to remind us of why we have acted in a certain way. In fact, we forget to ask who is actually in control. Who is really hiding behind the face: the one with the painting, or the painter, or both?

Often, what begins as a game quickly turns into a competition. "Let's see who is going to win," you say. Wilson gives you a run for your money and bounces around, going off course, and all you can hear is, "Loser!" Actually, that's exactly what you were trying to avoid feeling like or being perceived as: a loser. You had been unaware that, whilst chasing Wilson around, trying to kill time, you were in fact reaping the result of the seed sewn in avoidance: failing to look at a face with no mask. Instead, you introduce other rules, by painting on new tags from the long list of aliases, initiated by Wilson's godfather, which include self-pity, helplessness, hopelessness, regret, arrogance, loneliness, and procrastination, but best summed up as doubt.

As far as you're concerned, it's Wilson's fault that you've found yourself running too far and off course. Your intention to ensure that you are always aware of his whereabouts requires your constant engagement and participation in the games. He knows nothing else. This is because he was created in the concealment of your image and likeness. However, the moment you lose sight of Wilson because he happens to be somewhere in a corner, you become aware of the real state of your affairs. Your initial reaction of alarm and outburst gains you a ticket called reality check.

Evidently, you have been acting the fool; that is why you have not scored any goals. You still mull over the fact that you have not taken the opportunity to stand in front of a group or pay someone a compliment. The idea of learning a new language or taking an airplane ride is still left on hold. Furthermore, your son is still waiting for you to take him to the dressmaking class. What do you do? I'm a real jerk! you say to yourself, feeling like real a loser, too. So you decide to fetch Wilson. You make him a promise never to leave him again and then suggest another game. You want to win. "Okay, last game," you say. Of course, the game has been going on forever. Only this time, you have added another variable: to win because you think that winning will validate your idea of trying to kill time.

All along, you are unaware that you are actually being presented the chance to score an unexpected goal: the understanding that you don't need to feel so attached to Wilson, and he does not need constant interaction from you. The realisation that it's time for a change and embracing new opportunities for achieving your main goal is a huge goal in itself, but alas! You missed! So what do you do?

As you walk along, cursing yourself, you knock Wilson, Bap! Bap! Bap! on his head whilst he bounces up and down. Intermittently, you hold onto him with both hands and look at his face with a sense of self-pity, as if he were the sweetest child ever. Feeling sad, you wonder, Is he really?

"If you were really a sweet child, then why have you wasted so much of my time, making me chase you around?"
Your level of frustration is building sky-high. The game had gone well into overtime, not to mention how exhilerated you now feel, after running the whole nine miles, just to fetch him; you think to yourself, Plus, you didn't even win! All of a sudden, boop! With all

your frustration, you kick Wilson really hard, right between his eyes. The next thing you know is that thirty minutes later, you wake up with a pounding headache and hearing the words, "You've been in stillness! You've been knocked out!" After all that, you're still trying to figure out what really happened.

You had not taken into account that Wilson actually thrives on frustration; thus, finding something like himself in you, on which he could attach himself to: another face that looks like his godfather, Fear, the legend.

Generally, we tend to feel that we must always play with Wilson to ensure his happiness. Each time he runs off, we feel that we must catch him or fetch him because we must have him. However, we ought to realise that while we may feel the need to protect him, it is impossible to score any goals whilst holding onto the ball. Before then, we must be prepared to let go so that we can serve and score goals. Otherwise, we will inevitably be faced with the question: What happened? Why am I still lying here? As such was my case:

In 2005, I had gotten myself at the centre of an employment dispute. I had filed a complaint against my manager for his poor manners towards me, which followed my refusal to continue backdating health and safety checklists. That obviously meant filling in the lists with fictionalised figures. The fact that I had to sign my name to each list was a disturbing reminder of my involvement in a dishonest act. To resolve the matter, I was hoping that he would be seriously reprimanded or get fired altogether. Since he was a temporary worker, I did not think that would be difficult. As it turned out, the whole attention of that case boomeranged and knocked me out for six because he had filed a complaint against me for negligence – for not administering the pro re nata to a service user. In hindsight, I felt that what had appeared like a breakdown in communication between myself and another member of staff was actually a well-orchestrated conspiracy to have me fired. That meant I was under investigation whilst suspended from duties.

After my second interview in this investigation, I concluded that the policies and regulations were just cleverly written documents that allowed the more creative persons to prove their case as being right all along. However, my determination to expose the manager, and their insistence on firing me, had become a game of volleyball, while I thought that I was just playing catch. Subsequently, I just held onto the ball.

You get what you give more attention to …

In short, having Determination as my middle name, I held tight to the ball; I took unilateral action against the company, which seemed to pay little attention to my complaint because all their attention seemed focused on the case against me. Their idea was that since the manager was in a higher position to mine, it was not important that I should know the outcome of my complaint. That was, even though I was still experiencing ill attitudes at the time. Since I had no intention of backing down, and to avoid a court scandal that could damage their reputation as a care provider of services for vulnerable persons, the company offered me a settlement figure.

The second offer, which I accepted, included a clause that I must never use their name in any public matters that could prove detrimental to the organisation. Feeling very drained at the time, I accepted, with no hope or wish to ever speak of them. I was willing to let go of the ball. However, I was unaware that I had been knocked out and found it difficult to release my fingers from the arthritic position with which I had held onto the ball for so long. This was due to my attachments to the range of facial tags I had gained.

During that time, I barely smiled. I had worn the painted face of self-pity. I complained to everyone I knew about my dreadful plight: "Can you imagine, me of all people? These people have accused me of abusing the service users." And of course, the responses of alarm would further compound my conviction of victimisation, and so I went on.

I found myself consciously eating unhealthy foods because that's what depressed people do, I thought. I ended up piling on a mass amount of weight and telling myself, I'll shift it off when I'm ready. I certainly drank more alcohol than usual too, because, again, that is what depressed people do: I was holding firmly onto the ball. I was wearing the painted face of helplessness.

The case was over, and then came the big two-word question: "What next?" I was trying to understand what had hit me. Since I was no longer holding the ball, there was no longer that face to hide under. I realised that my arrogant face painting had been worn to prove myself dead right, as Dale Carnegie puts it in his book How to Win Friends and Influence People. Although I had read the book, I had not applied the principle in this case: the willingness to see the other's point of view, as well. I had lost my power to Fear because I was not using it. I was too busy holding onto the ball. I had failed to do the maths correctly and thought that having a mortgage equalled a hindrance to my personal development and self-esteem. I clearly suffered from the condition of Excusitis, a term coined by David Schwartz in Doing It Now, his book on overcoming the disease of procrastination (doubt) and failure in accomplishing your desires.

There I was, instead of allowing myself the chance that I knew, deep down, I deserved a more satisfying position. Instead, I pretended to be happy and contented whilst hiding behind the face of self-importance. And the fact that others were actually seeking my advice on the job provided me yet another face with which to hide. Despite the constant unreserved comments from some of my colleagues, that I should be operating a managerial position, I still held onto the ball with the face of Procrastination. How was I to drop Wilson, as if I were Mr Altidore, stepping into the tombed casket, just like that, whilst others were looking up to me? Could I risk being exposed? I needed to hide. I needed to hide my feeling that I was not good enough for what I really desired in my heart to do: show others how not to hide, by shining my light. So afraid, I hid behind the face of procrastination.

But hiding is hard work, with the constant seeking to cover up distortions.

In hindsight, I saw that the people I worked with appeared kinder to me than I previously thought. They were, in fact, covertly working in alliance with the Crimson Light, which was beckoning me to "Let go! Let go of the ball." They had actually been waving the red flag: "Time to take a reality check." Instead of paying attention, I took offence. Then it was time-out. I was out because I simply had been knocked out. Nevertheless, it still meant I would have to uncover each mask, even though I was faced with fear.

Why was I really forming the fool, running around with Wilson? I discovered that even though Wilson had been sweet and kind in his own way, he got bored over time, and I was unaware that the rules had been changed. I was unaware that while I wore the face of hopelessness, he had matched mine as regret, and the rules were never the same anymore because no one can hide forever.

Wilson had been whinging to Godfather Fear, "The game is not funny anymore." And that meant someone had not been paying attention to the rules. I had not understood that when Wilson runs far off course, just like in the case of Hanks, it means he wants out of the game. Like I wanted to see the results of my complaint, so was Wilson; he was determined.

Now Godfather Fear had worked very hard building his empire and thought it was time to relax, but he hardly got a chance to do just that, which means he got increasingly impatient. That is why he got angry with Wilson, participating in so many games and putting up with different faces. On the other hand, since we continue to find numerous ways in which to increase the numbers of participants and spectators, Godfather allowed the games. Still, he complained, "People and their silly games. Oh, did you see?"

"Watch later. I must see. It's a must-see. I could've, would've, should've seen". The Legend only allows the games because Wilson can always be kept busy.

Another thing about Godfather Fear: He does not like people repeating the same empty promises over and over in his head ("I will … I will …"), without any action. Actually, that is how I knew I had been hit by him whilst showing Wilson how to play the game at level three. That's the stage of "Stop talking in my head and do something. Do anything. That would be doing something." Perhaps this was the lesson Mr Barack Altidore had learned, so that he could complete the course "Why Be Afraid?" Otherwise, how would he have had the courage to step into the tombed casket, just like that?

It does make sense to do something. For instance, I once saw a huge dazzling light a little offside, towards the sunset. Then, I thought, What an amazing sight. Perhaps it's the end of the world, but how could it be? I have not yet reached the Bridge of Actualising Self-full Love and delivered my message to the world. I quickly concluded that it must be the moon on its way to kiss the sun. Whilst in full anticipation for the moment of eclipse, I wondered, What if I am wrong? I walked nearer towards the light, only to discover that it was the sun beaming on the glass door of a dilapidated car beside the nearby garage. Umm, that's Fear for you, always trying to get you to do something, I thought. I was no longer dazzled nor frightened because I had faced Godfather Fear, who had showed me a truth: "False Evidence Appearing Real" can instantly dissolve into the rays of the Crimson Light.

And there was yet another truth, as I stood positioned where the light had beamed onto the glass. See, who is dazzling now that I am standing in the rays of light? Must be me, I thought. I felt happy, since I had done something and had learnt how important it is for us to align ourselves in light of our hope and desires. Then, I thought,

Why be afraid to accomplish my mission and to act on the message that I want to deliver to the world? Fear is always pointing us to the light, but it would seem like one has to be barefaced and willing to stand in the same position as fear.

As I had anchored onto this lesson, I saw that it is imperative to always remember, maybe that is why Wilson loves to burst into a sweat, like when playing hide-and-seek, just to get you to do something. Meanwhile, his godfather just sits there, exactly where he knows you intend to hide. All you hear is, Boo! And the next thing, you are flat on the ground, wondering what happened, ensuring that you do something, even to pay attention to the lecture, "Why Be Afraid?"

Children of Regret and Doubt, whilst you're there trying to kill time, make up for lost time, and race against time, by saving time to watch it later because you think it is a must-see, pay attention. Since you can't run or hide forever, why not live honourably?

Prior to my case, I worked over two years for the same company and had refused several offers of joining the organisation on a permanent basis, even though my hours were still full time. I had no fear of being sick or not having enough money. Eventually, after listening to all the highlights of possible hindrances I could face, without holidays and sick pay benefits, and the pension scheme, I accepted a permanent offer. That meant I bought into the idea of belonging to an organisation by which I could be identified as gaining more credibility in society at large. The main idea for working flexible hours in the first place was, so that I could spend more time with my son, was now compromised due to the stringency of working hours. Another face was presented, and I just followed suit.

Truth always seeks to be expressed.
This is the wonderful thing about the Crimson Light: It never ceases to show up, regardless of what face you may choose to wear,

even though it may require the whole force of an organisation to help you do something.

This is how I knew the light had beckoned me on towards a higher plane. It was then I heard, "You have big dreams and aspirations, but why are you still holding onto the ball? Instead, why not live your dreams and make them real? Or don't you think they can be made real? If they couldn't, you would not have them at all."

The Crimson Light was showing me that it could melt away Fear, in a flash, and then hand me a trophy, just like that. It could match up to whatever I desired. It was teaching me that adversities are actual gifts of the Open University of Life, often in the shape of a ball. I learned that I could choose to play whatever game I wish, as long as I was prepared to let go so that I can serve not only myself but the world. So why be afraid?

Finally, I had to address my pain of the aftermath. Where was I exactly? I was recovering from an arthritis attack. I certainly didn't care too much for the chance of seeing Wilson's face all over the place or for the fact that I had gotten bruised and didn't win the game. However, I decided to keep Wilson just where I could recognise him, whilst I kept my mind on being healed. I had learned that even though I found a degree of refuge in hiding behind Wilson, I could always let go. It's okay to say pass, and it's not because I've been hit by the ball that I must catch it or have it. I can let go at any moment. Letting go is to be mindful that sometimes, the less attention given to Wilson and his Godfather Fear, the more attention is required to building faith to serve. I was now learning a whole new ballgame. I refreshed my mind with how to love myself, so why be afraid?

Ah, I knew that I had to pick myself up. I had to do something. In retrospect, I was able to appreciate the many benefits of that experience to help me restore balance in my life. I had been saved from being totally burnt out. I have to admit that, perhaps, I had fallen flat on my face. What I know for sure is, when you have been hit really hard by Godfather Fear, you just ache like hell, all over.

However, in the end, the pain had been my saving grace. I was able to let go of pretending that I was having a real ball and that the company could not do without me.

Parenting over the phone was no more; I was spending quality time with my teenage son. My neighbours, too, were pleased that they no longer had to put up with the noise of unauthorised parties. Reviewing my social life, I was able to reciprocate the joys of true friendship. Finally, I was able to examine another vital item on my to-do list: my husband, who constantly complained of not getting enough … God knows I was doing my best, which was not good enough, to even work out the simple equation of attention that could have perhaps saved our marriage. I was the vehicle, perpetually driven on reserve, that sometimes stalled halfway before reaching the intended destination. Of course, it did not take long for him to find another, on a full gas tank and firing on all cylinders. Our case ended like Hanks and Wilson: drifting away from each other on a bed of unpleasant emotions. The time had come; he had drifted too far, and I couldn't be bothered to fetch him, and so I knew that I had to let go, in order to rescue and reignite my zest for life.

I found a past list of goals and saw that I was able to cross nine out of ten items, and that was including a husband (even though we had ceased to exist as a couple). It works, I thought. Writing down my goals really worked for me, so why be afraid to look into the future?

My eyes were not fixed on the ball, even though I was consciously creating Wilma, Wilson's sister. She is very gentle. I needed tenderness, while I felt somewhat ashamed to move into the world.

I decided to enrol in a local community project for personal development that involved helping people discover their interests. I had loads of interests but needed confidence and a sense of purpose. I was too advanced for the practical skills they offered, including the introduction to information technology, but I needed direction. And sometimes, you must follow the rear view to go forward.

The course bore all the hallmarks of my last job. It was as though the Crimson Light had given me yet another chance to objectively review my situation, without all the emotional attachments involved. While I became mindful that others were looking up to me, I was not hiding anymore. Instead, I was just being barefaced, looking for direction on how to get to level three of "Why Be Afraid?"

The trainer, Helena, and I struck a good rapport. I had seen something in her like myself on which I could attach myself to becoming. She was doing a job that reminded me of exactly what I wanted to do: help people discover what they want to do, even though at the time, I had been faced with both sides of the coin. This time, I knew that I could simply put Wilma in a corner or roll Wilson down a hill; it didn't matter. I was focused on being real; I had faith to do something.

Through Helena, I was able to attend a four-day intensive course that allowed me to explore some deep-seated emotions. I was able to offload, like never before. I became new and was at peace with myself. I had faced Godfather Fear, barefaced, in a safe environment with a group of people I trusted. It was the beginning of acknowledging my inner power through the Crimson Light.

Financially, I had no idea exactly how much the course had cost. All I can say for sure, it required the release of a lot of pain, so I had to let go. However, I had enough of the stuff to wholeheartedly donate in full plus leaving a very huge tip, emotionally, because the Crimson Light had given me enough spirit.

> Through my trails of life's joys, dreams, and challenges
> Lay the shapes of the melting rays of the Crimson Light,
> The trophies that held me in high esteem.
> They represent the demarcation of every victory gained

And for each unit undertaken, "Why Be Afraid?"
A higher level of the unknown, that's Fear.
Yet still so near, like a niggling companion;
Another painted face awaits the revelation
Of the hour that I had slept in
Grazebrook Primary School:
A truth that revealed that there was still more pain
But more trophies yet to gain.

Like a bud, this wisdom to unfold;
I knew, because I was once again with Fear.
As I focused my attention on what would be revealed,
"That is fine; you can do one of two things:
Make sure you are moving in the direction of your goals,
And even with both hands on the ball, or
Remember there always comes a time
When you'll have to let go."
So I had been told.

Yes! Fear, my slave master,
Driving me onto the next level,
But has no idea while he is there in my head
I am led by the grand-master: The Crimson Light,
Therefore, I know I am safe in whom I am.
Yet it's a knowing that seems evident only at intervals
And gets absorbed through partaking
The sandwich of wisdom and understanding:
the module "Why be afraid?"

Consequently, as I browsed the outline of the next unit, for actualising self-full love, I noticed that it had not allowed much space for complacency. The sensations of pain were already taking hold of me. Feelings of restlessness and the groaning of despair felt like months, and even years, of repressive catharsis just waiting to be released.

I felt a long absence of Resignation and even old Chatterbox, too. They seemed to have given up on me. Perhaps my ears had become too faint to hear, for confusion and uncertainty had once more resurfaced. I was faced with doubt once again. Am I there yet? Or will I really get there on the Bridge of Actualising Self-full Love? Yet the courage to persevere was right there in my very tears. But somehow, I knew it was an invitation from the infirmary, Hope for the People (HPTP), that I should find the faith and relief of my pain. In that instant of knowing laid the teardrops that had merged with the melting rays of the Crimson Light and my calamities, and had formed beautiful trophies.

This in turn helped me conjure up sufficient strength in preparation for my next step. I knew the signs by now. I just had to consent to bear the pain of losing Wilson and even Wilma, too. I am now in expectation for my payoff, the main trophy onto the Bridge of Actualising Self-full Love.

So I would surrender to the Crimson Light that always beckoned me unto another …

A bronze for my physical fitness or silver for my spirit? Mind you, gold would be nice, for this had been long foretold, a real prize to behold! So why be afraid?

Once more, I repeated my mission statement:

"My mind is made up: I have measured the undertakings; I have counted the cost! It is with determination that I intend to joyously attain my desire of getting onto the Bridge of Actualising Self-full Love, thereby reflecting the beauty of the Crimson Light. This intention, or something better, now manifests for me in miraculous satisfying ways. Amen."

And like before were the words against my ear, "Keep on keeping on."

Anchoring Points

There are no accidents and no coincidences, but the choices we make:
Today, I am making a choice to be
present,
attentive, and
intentional.

I am now open and receptive to the guidance of the Crimson Light;
therefore, I am trusting the choice I have made to believe in
magic,
protection, and
freedom.

The Naked Splendour

The naked splendour of the Crimson Light cloaked me in the warmth of the morning sun; though I'm sore with grief, it encased my heart to the core. What splendour! What magic to unveil when the Crimson Light shone from within, where shame and guilt is no more the game, but rather a pure act of concealment by far exceeds secrets of great magicians, even that of David Blaine.

CHAPTER 2

A Mother's Consent to the Light

As I was going over the scene in my mind, I had another profound and penetrating thought, one with the assistance of my loyal friend, Resignation, a thought that I was obliged to act upon: It was about my son. A wrenching feeling in my gut had touched the very core of my solar plexus and threaded its way into my heart. I had an urge to cry out loud all that I had suffered and failed to have said: the long wishful conversations with my son. Not in the sentiment of the cards or video clips send to friends and loved ones, but I wanted to say, "Wish you were here," followed by a half-welcomed interruption. It was a message to my ears, as I listened to a familiar voice: "Did you not see the smoky black hole, including the two written pages of your diary? Why is it then that you do not see your son? Yes, he is here, even though you cannot see him with your naked eyes. You only need to close them and to remember that you are the mother of many sons. Furthermore, the power of the Crimson Light has provided you the right to utter your thoughts to be consciously valued as priceless presents, for that is what holds the power of life and death. Therefore, the good intention of your utterance is all you need right now, to reveal that which yearns within. Remember, they are no different than your prayers, meditations, and affirmations that you have earnestly exercised over time. Just allow the universe to take care of the rest."

That said, I sensed the nodding consent of Resignation again, as in my head, followed by the advice: "Just say the word and your soul shall be healed, and leave no room for resistance."

As though knocking on my heart's door, the voice continued, "Be certain to have faith. But know that faith without work is dead. It is only when you have demonstrated an act in accordance with your desire that you not only exercise faith but also your willingness to let go."

Then I reflected on all my previous rehearsals, for a much anticipated moment, that I would pay my loyalty to my dear son. I had failed because I needed to let go of doubt. Then, I found courage in the words, "Remember! I am with you always; just speak."

The constant playback of the man descending in the tombed casket, including his Eulogy, given by Chatterbox, seemed like déjà-vu. Only this time, I felt that I knew Mr Altidore. I could see his separate selves and even his childhood games; I've known his scent and blooming smile from birth, including the immense joy that beamed on his face when he heard the words, "Yes, you can walk to school on your own." I also knew he struggled with sporting games, since his father was too busy to care. I knew when he told a lie and when he spoke the truth, like when he was asked, "Have you been smoking weed?" His response was always a big fat "No!" And I knew that was a true lie.

His mind was sharp as a blade and his mouth like a fiery furnace. Even as a child, he empathised with those less privileged and wished that he could help, but the ambivalence he felt wrenched his heart, since, he wanted so much for himself. I knew when he had a fight and saw the fearful look in his eyes. Nevertheless, his life was one of joyous experiences too, like his first love, for it conveyed the essence of what made him smile even more. I knew him oh, so well.

I felt inclined to rest the blame on my long-term friend Chatterbox; his "attention-seeking deficit" seemed to have obscured my judgement of a truth that had been unveiled and now allowed me to see the child I bore within.

He was a lot like Mr Altidore, working daily with the dead, though he was not with corpses, but more about ideas and dreams, ideas that he had been learning to cosmetically package and hoped to sell, and as for dreams, he just kept striving for his ideal.

The voice whispered once more, "You are the mother of many sons, and remember, I am with you always."

I knew that I was approaching the Bridge of Actualising Self-full Love through the Crimson Light and was about to fulfil my deepest desire: the ultimate quest individuals must face to discover who they are becoming. And even then, I could not walk away from the pain that I had caused.

In my quest for solace, I saw that at the core of the Crimson Light lies a soft, ever so gentle beam that gleamed its reflection right through his heart. His heart had been encased with fear: the dread that no one cared. And the light immediately showed me that my presence had indeed been an act of faith, to help melt away the crystallised encasement of the once gentle heart. All I needed to do was follow the guidelines of the light that works, since it does not behave unseemly, nor does it seek its own power, and therefore, at its best, it operates on the frequency of love for our healing and liberation.

This realisation had caused me to feel something in him like myself that would help me consent to his pain, as I cried, "Son, it is with love that I am saying 'sorry.' It is by faith I trust that you'll forgive me. I am sorry for disappointing you in this life and for not being the mother you had hoped for. I know you felt let down and responsible for all your painful experiences, but none of this is your fault. This is certainly not what I wanted for you, although I acknowledge the time has come to make your own decisions on how you wish to see yourself in the world. Nevertheless, I am also aware that it does not end my role as a mother: your mother. I have also concluded that I can no longer continue my role behind secrets and lies, through which I have also discovered that without complete honesty and openness of who I truly am with you, my role as your mother would be nullified. Moreover, my son, I cannot go on further in my quest for the peace of mind I envisioned. I would have teach you all I possibly can."

I prayed many times for forgiveness of myself and of others, just to find peace. Still, the peace that I found seemed like droplets that have now rendered me a long list, reflecting the absence of its reign. Subsequently, I now seek the peace that provides a sense of deeper understanding: To breaking the cycle of the generational curse of disharmony in our family so that you won't have to endure the full impact of the pain and shame it has reared. My desire and experiences in the Open University of Life made me realise that continuing to avoid this matter could be detrimental to the personal growth and of all concerned.

On one hand, I thought I had been as honest with you as necessary, so I told you only what I thought you should know, whilst on the other hand, I endeavoured to protect you by withholding secrets and lies from you. The secrets, however, have impacted on me, as one whose back is now against the wall. I now see how the lies have rippled and influenced my judgement as a woman and as a mother, including the pluses and minuses. I am now aware that unless I own up to my mistakes and my truths, including my dreams and aspirations, I would remain stagnant, even though we know that nothing is obsolete, especially since life always presents us opportunities to be in conscious motion. For this reason, however, instead of waiting to get hit by a bus or have some great catastrophe thrust upon me, I have now chosen my path: to go along with the source of the Crimson Light, which beckons me onto the Bridge of Actualising Self-full Love.

As Emmet Fox puts it, there are many roads to the Crimson Light, some easier than others, but love, he claims, is by far the easiest of all. That is why I have now devoted my energies to the dance of love.

The Crimson Light taught me that without the art of attaining self-full love, I will be nowhere, get nowhere, because without a vision in mind, I would be like a lost sheep, with absolutely no idea of where I could be or mean to be going. I learnt that many people at the Open University of Life face the tough class only after a terrible ordeal, often to wake up to the words of a stranger telling them where they are, because they had no idea. The Crimson Light teaches that the reason for one's existence is to take sole responsibility for her own salvation. I want to be saved, and I want you to be saved also.

Is there ever a right time for confession, or a right time for atonement? I don't know apart from when it feels right.

Son, what I have to say may hurt and may cause you to feel resentment towards me, but the song of love is playing the tune that requires us to dance. You see, all of life is a tune and a dance. Therefore, let the utterance of your cries and your joys be our song and let the wells of our emotions be our dance. By this understanding, we would demonstrate our acts of faith for that which we seek, ensuring to always keep love in mind and heart.

Though my knees continued to shiver, I no longer remained seated, since I obliged the request of my soul. Regardless the outlook of a deeply dreaded tune, I got up and danced. With bended knees and broken from within, I now gave my consent to the Crimson Light. Come on, son! Let's dance; never mind my swaying steps.

Son, I would rather if I could skip the stories and just tell you what I have learnt. However, I am aware that the things I learnt were really my lessons, and all may not serve you well. Therefore, I can only express my God-given gift to tell it like it is. In addition, I believe this also marks the point of my nearly ending quest, so let's begin.

There was a time in my early twenties, I had allowed myself to be subjectively entertained by Chatterbox, and subsequently, I almost lost my mind. It was the result of my embarrassing dark thoughts and feelings of killing my own self. I gave up on the idea after finding out that the options of my potential exit were too depressing to consider, in my quest for a painless death. By what I had seen on television, I thought that a cocktail of tablets was a safe option, but I hated the idea of being found in a state where I would have to be pumped up. I certainly could not do the knife thing, either.

Chatterbox kept yapping in my head, reminding me, like he often did, about what my stepfather Mr All-Bags-full had said: I would not amount to anything good. He said by the time I was fourteen years old, I would get pregnant, and I would be of no good use to anyone, not even myself. To make matters worse, that feeling was compounded when my biological father called me a slut and told me that I could never survive in the big world on my own. Although a part of me was constantly trying to prove them wrong, I was still left confused and frustrated. My dreadful behaviours, on occasion, would easily tip the scale that would prove them right.

For example, my first pregnancy was when I was about eighteen years old. Although not fourteen as prophesied, life had handed me a cloak of shameful feelings of hopelessness and helplessness. This had shaped my early childhood belief that I was probably born to suffer and that my existence served no good purpose on this earth. Ultimately, I had little, if any, sense of self-worth.

That pregnancy was by my brother-in-law Spenks, whom I had just come to know. The affair with Spenks happened very early on my second arrival in England (the first was in my mother's belly). Of course, I had no recollections of people or places then. From there, I went on to continue my formative years in St Lucia, where I remained until that second trip. Son, that experience alone could have ended Chatterbox's life (and, of course, mine too).

I was so distraught to know that something of life was growing inside of me. Sorry to tell you, son, but I was planning a termination of the six-week-old foetus. Not knowing my situation at the time, my sister Lorraine related a horrible incident that she had learnt through the media. It was about a young woman who tried terminating her pregnancy with a fork and consequently bled to death. That option, for me, was immediately ruled out, though I felt that I understood the desperation of the lady in question. Instead, I tried heaps of laxatives, including Epson salts, but nothing happened. Before I move on to explain more about the pregnancy, let me give you some background into how all this came about.

It was in the early autumn when I arrived in London, and everything was new to me. So new that the closest I had ever been to a television, prior to that, was passing the window by the local photographer in Micoud Village. Apart from the fact I spent some of my growing years there, it's also where my siblings and I attended school.

I was picked up from the airport by my father and his best friend, a black cab driver named Freddy, both of whom I was meeting for the very first time. I was like a little child, feeling totally ecstatic with pride and joy, an absolute delight, for the day I had so longed dreamt about had come. This is it! Just like I imagined him to be, I said to myself, just as I thought. I could feel my cheeks bursting with delight. Let me tell you, son, my dad was well-groomed in his suit and tie, looking intelligent and wearing glasses; I felt so proud. He seemed very welcoming of my presence too.

That void that I grew up with for many years was no more. It was a very fulfilling moment. I felt safe. It was then that I was taken to live with Lorraine, the eldest of five legitimate sisters. I was often referred to as illegitimate because my father was not married to my mother; that's how I knew what illegitimate meant.

Father ensured that my welfare was well taken care of, which he generously replenished on his weekend visits. Back then, Lorraine and I shared the same Christian name. I got the impression that sharing the same name (we were referred as little and big or number one and two) was indicative of a strong connection; we had more than blood in common, and that led us onto a good path. Lorraine and her husband had only one child, Bernadette, about seven years old. Bernadette was the prettiest little girl I had ever seen. She seemed to have everything I attributed to a beautiful doll, even though she was not quite as white.

Their family's warm receptivity of my presence made me feel welcomed. On the other hand, I also felt rejected, as my other sisters bluntly expressed no wish to see me. Somehow, their curiosity got the better of them, and they phoned to inquire about my features. I could hear Lorraine say, "She's very pretty, but very skinny." It was not just her, but it seemed that all those who saw me said the same, with the use of the word "undernourished." That led to me being encouraged to eat, as though I were a cow being fattened in preparation for slaughter. "Skinny," for me, soon replaced "rude," which had been a label that I had acquired for being outspoken. Being called rude was also attributed to the fullness of my lips. The cultural belief was that if your lips were full or pouted, that definitely meant you were rude.

Both skinny and rude had become the criteria for me being mocked by Spenks. He developed a habit of flapping my bottom lip.

He ensured to apply enough pressure that would create a trembling sound on impact with my upper lip, as though they hadn't been slapped enough, I used to think.

He would say, "What's up, rubber lips?" This term, too, had replaced the "cupped rim" by which my former schoolmates teased me, but that was in reference to the width of my mouth.

I was often caught off guard by Spenks in these acts of entertainment. How could I get him to stop? I often felt tired of expressing my disapproval, which just seemed to fall on deaf ears. Trying to maintain a serious composure was not easy either because he would tickle me, and of course I would end up laughing until I would beg to go to the bathroom. Even to this day, it is difficult for anyone to get me laughing in this way. The experience had progressively helped me to build my defence mechanism. However, I had lacked the must-add ingredients necessary that would affirmatively demonstrate my wish to have him stop. Moreover, I did not want to be seen as rude to new people and in a new place.

Carrying on with their normal lives, both Lorraine and Spenks worked full-time, whilst Bernadette attended school. That meant I was home alone until I found a job. The situation had furnished the perfect opportunity for what followed on. The couple gave me a telephone number, in case I had any concerns at all. I could call my brother-in-law, who worked nearer home, a ten-minute drive away. As it turned out, after experiencing a fear of noises from the basement, I followed the instructions. Spenks arrived, went halfway down into the basement, and returned to get me to come along and see for myself if there really was anything there. I reluctantly went with him, and we both concluded that there was nothing there to fear.

The following day, as usual, everyone kissed each other goodbye as they went their separate ways, a practice that I had not even dreamt of but admittedly liked, because to me, it meant love. However, it turned out on that particular morning, Spenks pushed his tongue right up my mouth, even with my sister standing just a couple feet away. I went straight into shock. From there on, Spenks would often return home because he'd conveniently forgotten something.

I was raped the first time in the hallway of the terrace house, which he later confessed was so that he could see through the glass door if someone was coming. To have his way with me, Spenks insisted that I had called him that day because that was what I wanted, forcing himself on me and insisted that I was going to have "it." All this was happening just over one month or so of my arrival. It didn't matter that I cried my eyes out, telling him to stop because that was not what I wanted and that he got it all wrong, but he forced his way on me anyhow. I admit that he was kind of good looking and at times funny, but what he implied was untrue. More so, there were many things I did not like about Spenks, apart from flapping my lips; he was a wife beater who sat on his butt and would just make endless demands. He reminded me of your grandfather, Mr All-Bags-full. Spenks was the type of man who thought making a cup of tea or pushing a shopping trolley was not a manly thing to do. He would rather wait in the car until such a female act was done.

Forcing himself on me became a habit. Several times, I tried to fight him off of me; even with tears rolling down my eyes, begging him to stop, it only seemed to turn him on more. Then, with Resignation, I gave in. After some time, I, in turn, decided to enjoy him. However, I was constantly terrified, not only because I knew Spenks was my sister's husband, but it just felt wrong, and I was terrified of getting pregnant as well. All I had was to trust his withdrawal techniques. Although eighteen, I knew little about contraceptives then.

Fear accompanied by glimpses of thrills became the thrust for our sexual encounters. Spenks would have me wherever and whenever there was a sign of opportunity. If there wasn't, he would create one. He was thoroughly obsessed and would even touch me when my sister was nearby, as though exclaiming the power he had over my lack of defences. He warned me that if I tried to avoid him, as I was attempting to do, Lorraine would become suspicious of my behaviour, so I should act normal. That meant he continued to tickle and wrestle with me and flap my lips, just to avoid her asking questions.

The rush grew progressively more exciting, but the guilt far outweighed the sexual gratification (perhaps because it lasted much longer). "We've got to stop this!" I would say to Spenks, but the words became like a broken record to his ears. The more I repeated myself, the guiltier I felt, but the more forceful and excited Spenks would become.

A part of me knew that I could stop, but how? Just asking him to stop was simply not enough. Instead, he rode on my timidity and lack of self-esteem. I had not demonstrated an act of faith in my defence or in the direction of my desire to stop. I felt powerless. On several occasions, I threatened to tell my sister, but Spenks managed to convince me otherwise. He said, "Lorraine and I have been together for a long time; what makes you think that she is going to believe you over me? If you are that mad to tell her, I will just tell her that you are the one who came onto me, and in any case, she hardly knows you. Furthermore, it would look worse on your part."

"Why?" I asked.

"You would be called a slut, What's a slut? I asked. A Jamet (creole term). But I, being a man, this would simply add more feathers to my cap, particularly amongst my friends."

And when it came to friends, Spenks had many. Even though this argument arose many times, I felt that he was right, and I did not have a leg to stand on. It would be just like I had been ridiculed in an interview by the police in St Lucia, when a young man attempted to rape me. He was found guilty as charged, but his whole family, who lived across the road from me, had turned against me. I was constantly taunted as the evil one. I would not wish to experience such humiliation again, so I was convinced Spenks was right.

Son, I was so disgusted with myself. I started spending a lot of time in the local West Ham Park, in East London; that's where I found solace. I loved the flowers, and they seemed to smile at me, a contrast to being indoors around people I felt I had betrayed. Behaving commonly towards them was proving too challenging.

When I realised that I was pregnant, I hated Spenks, though I felt a sense of relief that at least it would mean the end of us. I was petrified and was feeling even more helpless than ever. Spenks schooled me in how to handle the situation with Lorraine. He told me the exact words to say. He told me that I should convince his wife that the boyfriend I had left in St Lucia had impregnated me, even though I had a period since being in the UK. A woman having a period whilst being pregnant was news to me, but Lorraine confirmed that possibility. I felt doubly worse that I had now engaged her in the lie. Sadly, she was the only female and family I could rely on to help me. I couldn't relate the extent of my plight to a loving sister, who had expressed nothing but kindness towards me. Son, I feared the worst thing had happened: to have gotten impregnated out of wedlock, and shamefully, to my sister's husband; this thought nearly drove me insane.

The pregnancy test proved positive, and I was feeling relieved. That was until Lorraine asked me, "What will you do?"

"About what?" I asked.

"Well, the test said positive. Are you going to keep it? If you don't want to have it …"

It was then I realised that I gotten confused with the term "positive." As far as I was concerned, positive was what I wanted, and negative was what I did not want.

I suffered tremendous guilt and immense shame, compounded with the religious beliefs about acts of fornication and adultery, and my disloyalty to my sister, whom I actually liked. What would my mother say if she knew? What would people say? All that simply felt like too much to bear. If only I could find a hole big enough to bury myself in at the time, that's where I'd be. I found myself just like the Psalmist, King David.

> My heart and my flesh cried out;
> Streams of rivers run down my face
> And at night I soaked my pillow.

I was so desperate to get rid of what was inside me. In her loyalty towards helping me, and following Spenks' request if she knew anything that could help my case, Lorraine told me that she had heard jumping from the tabletop can cause a miscarriage, so I tried this several times, for several days, but to no avail. All I knew, I just had to have it out.

Lorraine accompanied me to the hospital, where the termination was scheduled, but the date seemed too far off. I would not be at peace until it was out of me. So periodically, I would hit my belly and continue to pray and wish it out.

I had not realised that I could endure physical pain that seemed equally intense as what I had experienced emotionally. That was, until the contractions and pangs had me screaming insanely as I bawled on the kitchen floor. It was as if the foetus knew that this was not a game, and if it was, then I was determined to win, but it would make me pay. I just wanted him out. It was as though he, too, had been raped. Anyway, I had a miscarriage that Sunday, which was one day before I was due to go into hospital for the termination. Son, just like you, too, began to make your way out into the world on a Sunday, the day before I was due to go in for a Caesarean section. Strange as it may seem, I felt that that experience with Spenks had confirmed all that had been said about my life.

Eventually, after some time, I found a job, and no more hitting myself. The Crimson Light was always showing a glimmer of hope.

I developed my love for fashion, learning to make coats in a factory. There, I learnt to engage and broaden my interest in people and places.

In ensuring my attachment to live up to the labels that had been plastered over my forehead, and as if to add credibility to the threat of ownership I felt Spenks had held over my head, one night, I kissed a family friend whilst he slept in a chair overnight. It might have been the fact that apart from being very handsome and looking so blissful that morning, I found attractive, or the fact he showed no interst in me. I am still not sure exactly why. He made a complaint. to Lorraine, which I denied, but that further tipped the scale of my unworthiness. It was like accepting a false passport; you become who it says you are. Consequently, I knew that I had been the subject of everyone's discussion, which further proved my sense of unworthiness amongst both family and friends.

Eventually, I got myself a boyfriend, who my sister thought was nice. Well, he took me out most weekends and bought me gifts. Everyone around us knew he kept another woman at home. That seemed fine, since he appeared happy to show me off to his friends. It was something to do.

Spenks, on the other hand, would not leave me alone, until one day Bernadette walked in on us. She screamed and ran out to her mother outside the front door, as though she had seen a ghost. It had not been an x-rated act, but it was enough for her to see how inappropriately we were kissing. Then I knew for sure I had to get out. I was not good to anyone, not even myself, as Chatterbox had reminded me. Lorraine threatened to leave, whilst Spenks tried to convince her of his love and that she should stay. "It's not what you think it is: It was she who came onto me! She is not worth it! Don't let us lose our marriage over her." Half-wishing there was someone to answer on my behalf, since my self-esteem was too low to disagree,

I could not make sense of such insulting remarks. Furthermore, I was tired.

All the people around us were told about what had happened. From there on, I felt embarrassed and judged by everyone, with the exception of Father, who seemed sympathetic to both Lorraine and me. However, his expression suggested, "Surely, anyone could have seen that coming, the way those two were wrestling and carried on." Father seemed more eager to express his distastefulness towards Spenks' sentiment and comments that it was not worth losing his marriage over me and I meant nothing to him. Father seemed to show the sense of equal value towards all his children. There was one thing for sure: Neither Spenks nor me were ever able to convince anyone that it was the first time.

I can't see why after that I needed to convince Father that I had to leave and find somewhere else to stay. I felt that to substantiate my wish, it was necessary I make a full confession to my friend: my father, turned priest, my all-in-one.

A few days later, I proceeded to tell Father all about Spenks, and I also took the opportunity to tell him about my stepfather, your grandfather, Mr All-Bags-Full, who had molested and physically abused me. I even told him how I had the job to empty out his poop from a pail, which I termed a "treasure pot." I insisted that I should leave my sister's home. From there on, I went on to share Uncle Paul's one-bedroom flat on Camden Road, North London. There, I was able to appreciate the wonderful innovation of a folding bed that was also used as a dining table, which meant I slept in the dining stroke living room.

A short while after, I received a letter from Mother, calling me a Jamet: the Creole term for slut, stating that I was sleeping with her brother. I wrote back, "If that is what you have to tell me, I would rather you do not write to me anymore." I had something pitiful to anchor onto: "Now, Uncle, even you can see for sure how unlucky I am. You can see that even Mum hates me! How come she never sent you a letter? Why she sent me one and not you?"

I was hoping that Uncle Paul would be at least half as angry as I was, since his name had been implicated, but he did not seem bothered at all. In fact, all my hopes for thinking that he would speak up on my behalf dissolved like salt in hot water. My only real friend was my father and my cousin Rebecca, who had a host of issues trying to integrate with her family and into a new society, like I was.

A few months later, my father suggested that I share his three-bedroom semi-detached house in Stoke Newington, near where I worked. It was more convenient for having somewhere to freshen up after work and jump onto the 73 bus route to attend my modeling course in West London. Uncle's girlfriends were not comfortable with my presence, and that often restricted them to the bedroom, so I moved in with Father. That way, I not only pleased the people who thought I should be a model, but also Uncle's girlfriends and Father, of course.

Apart from dancing, Father's social life was the pub, and he would often insist I come along. He always seemed happy to introduce me to people, who seemed eager to comment how beautiful I was. Even then, I don't ever recall being comfortable meeting all these strangers and drinking lager and Shandy. Perhaps comfort was something I never really knew, anyway.

Over time, I discovered that my father had a problem with me having male friends. There was always a host of questions being asked, and I would feel exhausted and guilty, like I had done something wrong, without knowing exactly what that was. His body language often said it all, and he refused to talk to me on several occasions.

One day, Father told me, "It is not safe for you to continue to occupy the room in which you sleep." When I asked why, he explained that his estranged wife was still coming into the house in our absence, and I could be hurt.

"What can I do? I just left Uncle's house. I can't go back now!"

"No. You will have to share my room; you'll be alright."

He convinced me of the potential harm, and Father showed me a letter that he had gotten through the post. It was from a woman who lived in Castries, the capital of St Lucia. I had no idea at the time that my father was illiterate. The fact he wore glasses made it unexpected. He asked me to read it out loud, and I did. The sender requested personal items of mine. "Make sure to send the girl's panty or brassiere, and her whole name and her date of birth. I will do the work as soon as I get it."

As it happened, a few days later, some of my clothes had actually gone missing from the garden line (but no underwear was included). I had not taken the threat seriously. The absence of physical contact would have made it impossible to do me wrong, and people can only hurt you if you've done them wrong, I thought, even though people like Mr All-Bags-Full and Spenks had hurt me without me doing them any wrong.

My father's request to abandon the room felt far more uncomfortable than the letter itself. The thought of going back to Uncle was uncomfortable, too. So I suggested to my father that we put a lock on the bedroom door, which was previously occupied by their last daughter, who was just be a few months older than me. He said that she still had rights to her room, and that was not the wisest thing to do. Nevertheless, I chose to believe that he had my best interest at heart; what could I say? My father was able to convince me that I would not be safe otherwise. Putting aside my awkward feelings, I accepted that my one and only friend seemed to be demonstrating care for me in a way that I had not known. I forced myself into thinking, Perhaps trusting someone is meant to feel awkward. Since I had opened up to him, revealing all my fears and guilt, too, I thought that I would be safe. My father would protect me, so I shared his room.

Sleeping next to my father felt extremely uncomfortable, as balancing my slender frame on the edge of the bed had me feeling rigid, as if I were a stick. I felt guilty for feeling uncomfortable. After all, he is nothing like Mr All-Bags-Full and Spenks, I thought. Perhaps people here just do things differently; everybody's kissing and hugging. Shortly after that, it became evident that my stepmother and my sisters were indeed trying to harm me.

One day, my stepmother and three of my sisters came to the house whilst I was cooking, and they taunted me. I was subjected to a long string of verbal abuse. They said that I had had several abortions, even before I arrived in England. My stepmother said, "You are even sleeping with your father," which I took little offense to because it was true. I was sleeping with my father, but just literally sleeping on the same bed. Furthermore, I didn't know all the implications of the term "sleeping with someone" and exactly what she was implying then. I was called a homewrecker, and they said that I had come to take all their husbands away from them. I ignored them, until Brenda, whose room I had occupied, threw a glass at my head, striking me over my eyebrow. It broke against the wall. I was scared. My eye that had been missed went stright into shock. Since they were evidently greater in number and force, I held out the knife that I was using and approached Marian, who was holding a baby. I went for the weakest link, of course, with no intention to harm either one, and was hoping they would run away. Instead, they panicked, and began to scream saying "'Oh my God! Oh my God you crazy! You mad!" The three voices were shouting in all directions as they rushed around me, and unto the floor; each directing the other what to do."take the knife from her!", We all ended up in a struggle (just like the struggle with the man who was trying to rape me). I could not afford to let go of the knife, for fear that they would harm me with it. I suppose they had the same concern about me, too. However, the struggle ended after my stepmother slid her fingers onto the blade, and blood started pouring down. Even the next door neighbour came to see what was going on. I could not tell who'd let him in but in the end we had all found ourselves near the front door.

A few months later, I was charged with assault. In hindsight, I learnt that not having a voice is a sin and should also be a crime, especially when you are as timid as both my solicitor and I were. The judge said that by law he had to fine me, on the basis that I had admitted it was the knife that had caused the harm. He told them that it was evident that they had clearly gone to the house to harass me. He also said that he wished that he did not have to charge me, even though it was the minimum cost. After saying all that, he continued to ask me over and over, "Are you sure that this knife was the same knife you had in your hand," to which I repeatedly said, "Yes."

"Are you sure that that knife was the same knife that cut Mrs Grandville's finger?"

"Yes."

"Are you certainly sure that it happened whilst you were holding the knife?"

"Yes." In hindsight, I realised that he was hoping I would convey a shadow of a doubt, but I had not learnt the difference between people who were for me and those who were against me. Now then, with all this going on, it was evident I needed to feel safe.

Whilst preparing to go on a date one day, my father boldly said to me, "If it is that you feel you must have someone, I could be that someone, you know."

"What did you say?"

"If it is that you feel you must have someone, I could be that someone," he repeated.

While I found it difficult to believe my ears, his brazen attitude led me to believe that perhaps I was the one making a big deal out of what I was sensing to be so wrong. However, I still found the courage to remind him that he was my father and that is certainly not what I expected of him.

"I told you all that I had gone through with people taking advantage of me," I said, "and you are still saying something like that?"

Father calmly remained in his seat, and in the same tone as though he was just talking about the weather, he said, "I understood all that you told me about your mother's husband and Spenks, but let me tell you something: I am no different from any of them; that's just how men are."

Trying to work out my escape from the situation, I said, "I must go. I have to leave."

"Go where?"

Father insisted I needed him to protect me and said that I could never cope on my own. He said, "I am just another man, like any other man; that's how men are."

Whilst this might have been true, I felt perhaps that's what all women are expected to endure; otherwise, they would risk being sent away, just like Aunty Jocelyne and Yvonne. Furthermore, maybe that is why I was sent to live with different people as well.

It was like Spenks all over again, apart from the fact Father was older and more persistent in his use of subtle techniques, including emotional blackmail, such as, "If you love me, you would let me touch you."

I was faced with the dilemma that I had in fact become dependent on Father's tactile nature that confirmed his affection was all the love I had and had dreamt many years. On the other hand, it was too much to be constantly thinking about how to avoid him and how I would be without him. Yet it was all I thought about.

After many successful rejections, I can only assume being emotionally blackmailed was what validated my tolerance of Father on top of me. I felt even more powerless than I did with Spenks. I could not threaten to tell his wife or anyone else, for that matter. The only difference was that I spent more time resisting. Unfortunately, I still had not learnt that if you keep doing the same thing in the same old way, with the same mindset, you can only expect to get the same result. To make matters worse, I had not known that you can resolve matters by yourself. Sometimes, to make a change, all we need is something or someone to believe in. I did not feel I had that. Consequently, I was always looking for something or someone, outside of myself.

Some months later, I got pregnant by my boyfriend, a married man who claimed to be separated from his wife. He denied that it was his; he could not have impregnated me, he said. But some things you just know. I knew it was his from the very moment it happened, and I think Father had gotten tired of me pushing him off me. So I just knew.

When I told my father (slash friend and whatever else he was then) of my situation, what did he say? "You cannot keep it. You have to get rid of it; they will say it's mine."

At that point, Father told me that his wife had told everyone that we were sleeping together: a costly way of learning what "sleeping together" meant. Now, since I had it entrenched in my head that I did not want to be like Mother, raising a child without the actual father, like I had been, it was an easy decision to make. That way, it would not have to face a miserable life like mine. Under the umbrella of pregnancy, my feeling sick of life and sick of being me was intensified. I quickly had an instant termination in one of London's back-street clinics. Afterwards, I felt a sadness that confirmed I had consented to the belief that this is my life. It was a feeling like being at a department store with some bogus reason for returning an unwanted item; you knew you didn't want it in the first place, but you just bought it.

Sex had faded with Father, but not without mental and emotional struggle. Perhaps my persistence on late nights out helped, or maybe it was the big issue of relocating that was about to take place, but Father seemed to stop bothering me. It was nearing the close of the sale of the property; I finally saw a way out. The tiredness of constantly feeling dirty might have helped me develop enough courage. I felt strong. I told Father that I was determined to find somewhere to live on my own. Despite the thought I could not cope on my own, as he kept ringing over and over in my ears, I insisted. He knew that I knew that he knew I was serious. I was playing a different tune in a different way. You see, sometimes your back has to be against the wall to see that there is nothing left but possibilities. Then, he suggested buying an apartment for me. "Where would you be living?" I asked.

"Well, I'll stay with you, but it will be yours. It would be like compensating you for all the time you had no support from me as a child," he claimed.

I decided that I would not compromise my wish to end this in favour of material value. I wanted out, just as I wanted Spenks's seed out of me. I could not afford the thought of such luxury wrapped in misery. I just wanted it stopped for good. I was tired of feeling as though I were a bathroom and pretty much like dealing with Mr All-Bags-Full's treasure pails all over again. I was feeling dirty, so dirty that if I could have performed a "do it myself" exorcism, I would have. I am not sure whether I had developed any confidence to cope on my own or to cut ties, but I was determined to try.

I began having crazy thoughts: thoughts of stripping naked and running into the street, as though declaring to the world, "Look, I have nothing left to give, gain, or lose." I can only say, at that time,

I had definitely rubbed shoulders with insanity. What stopped me? I was able to capture a clear picture, as though in slow motion, that spelt out the message, "Who cares?" And then I saw that I would be left with my delusions as people watched but still carried on about their businesses. They would declare, "She's just gone completely insane," so in that instant, I consented to the Crimson Light to be still.

Then, there was the dream that one day I will be rich and happy, but I will also be gentle and kind to others. I wasn't sure how men would fit in that equation of kindness, but I would treat people nicely. There must be a way to be kind to others and maybe they too, will be kind to me in return, I used to think. Sanity had got me dreaming again. I would make it big as a model, but how? Since my confidence was very low, I would spend time trying to disguise the scars caused by Mr All-Bags-Full, including the many falls. They were too many, all over my body, although somehow, someone thought that I looked healthy enough to be featured naked in a health magazine. I still didn't feel good enough. Yet I was the perfect picture of health. I saw that I was strong enough to be able to shift from insanity to sanity.

As though raising my voice, "I will only agree to this on one condition: that this thing stops right now!"

"Okay, I agree."

In that moment, I felt that I had grown so much that I was like his mother. I later discovered that he could not have financed a mortgage solely on his income. Basically, there was a great deal of ignorance on my part. We got to the paperwork for the deed of sale, and it was then he disclosed his intention that I should have only 30 percent ownership instead of 50 percent, by law. Since I felt strong and in need of somewhere to stay, I accepted his lame deal. Later, I realised that my father had no intention of keeping his promise and was still seeking sexual favours from me. As much as he tried, I stood my ground. I had his word to use against him. I was able to say, "But you said! You promised."

The relationship became very sour, so much so that people around us could not understand why we argued so much. It was often said that we were more like man and wife, instead of father and daughter. Since I had no form of appropriate reference for either, I did not know how else to behave. Consequently, Father resorted to abusive behaviour and called me a slut. I should not have stayed out so late, even though it was only ten at night.

"You are the one who made me a slut," I responded.

I had never seen him this angry. He slapped me right across my face, pow! This happened on two separate occasions. I had to leave.

I left the house but soon found myself back after I broke up with my boyfriend.

Father could not wait to utter the dreaded words: "You see? I told you so!"

I must admit, I did wonder if I was able to really "cope in the big wide world," as he would often put it. However, a little voice whispered, "Keep the faith."

Since I had tested the waters, so to speak, I would keep trying until I succeeded, even if it meant several attempts, like I did before I could leave Mr All-Bags-Full's treasure pail in the baking sun. The Crimson Light would help me find the way.

Yes, maybe it was something to do with the solemn and self-pitying tune that I immersed my emotions in, marinated by the coarse sound of Lee Marvin singing "I Was Born under a Wandering Star" in Paint Your Wagon. I had learned this tune during my time with Spenks. I had not understood that all one's actions, including the beats that she listens to, are like sowing seeds that form the coins we exchange for items: Singing and dancing to sad tunes meant that is exactly what I was planting, and therefore my life was harvesting sadness and misery, thus having to endure the ripple effects of the exact thing I wanted to eliminate from my life. I planted yet more seeds of sadness.

If I could, I would dive to the bottom of the ocean; if I could fly, I would remain up in the sky; if I could drive, then I would go far away. Perhaps I will drive, I concluded. Another sad song would have me facing another challenge, with the instructor's hand up and down my leg whilst driving. I was moving in circles, the same circle on the same roundabout. The only difference was that I was actually paying someone my hard-earned cash to sexually harass me. That was clearly not adding up. By then, due to their frequent visits to Father, most of my sisters were on talking terms with me, and some of them even appeared to like me. I overheard one of them say, "I like the idea you always know where you stand with her; she's not a hypocrite."

I liked that description of me. I felt that it was generous and honest. They also seemed proud that I had undertaken such a brave thing that none of them did then: learning to drive.

Consequently, I was encouraged by one of my sisters to switch to her husband's driving school. He was another man with the notion that I owed him sexual favours. I was definitely over-facilitative; so much so that he displayed no reservations in demanding, "I want my share of what Spenks got from you." The audacity of his behaviour reflected a clear indication of my inability to differentiate between the obligation I felt and the empathy that I craved. The intertwinement of these factors subsequently left me enacting the distant phrase, "Whatever," especially for the fact I did not have a tombed casket to step into.

Though very unhappy, I continued to rely on the preference of sad tunes played by Chatterbox; that was why I almost silenced him for good, a second time, since I felt that I was born under a wandering star.

In my early thirties, whilst you were in St Lucia after the break-up with your father, I had fallen head over heels in love with

Hamilton, a Jamaican man who had another woman. I found myself once more in a situation that was nothing but drama. I was driving home after a huge fight with him, when he referred to me as "crazy." After he had gotten out of the car, I pondered on what he said; perhaps it was also how I felt. I thought of losing total control and crashing the car, hoping to kill myself. But then I thought, I have no guarantee that I would be dead, and if unsuccessful, I could end up having regrets and, perhaps end up in a wheelchair. The thought that really impacted on me was that this would be a terrible story to tell my son. The tears were streaming down my face, and at that moment, I prayed:

"God, forgive me that I have entertained such a silly notion. God, even if it means that I never find love again, please teach me how to love my son."

That came straight from my heart, and from there on, I consented to the Crimson Light. Loving you became my quest.

Subsequently, I felt that one of the greatest ways of being conscious of love was gained by having you. Having you allowed me the chance to manifest wishes and desires I might not have otherwise dreamt. It is as though you and I were intentionally role-playing actualising self-love. I did not know what love truly is, but through your smiles and the look in your eyes, the Crimson Light taught me the tremendous value of unconditional love.

The reciprocal gestures manifested in ways that not only enriched me but empowered me immensely. I knew I loved you for all eternity, and in some ways, I loved knowing that I was capable of loving and being loved because I had given my consent to the Crimson Light, which gave me the gift of life, even through you. I felt really good in my belief that I was nominated and had consented for this wonderful position of parenthood. It also gave me greater joy when, at eight years of age, you told me that you had indeed chosen me for your mother. I felt so good to have been chosen out of the billions of people in the world. Overall, I relished the view that I was the recipient of respect and responsibility for being your mother. I felt good.

Son, as you know, I did not always get it right. Frankly, there were times I wished there were a manual that I could follow on parenting. Due to my inability to ease your distress and your penetrating cries that seemed to go on endlessly, I felt bewildered inside. Chatterbox, too, was carrying on, and then one day, I cried out for help because I feared that I would go insane. I feared that I had been given too big a job and was proving myself incompetent. I felt hopeless. An instantaneous response occurred when my friend Stevenson stepped in through the door: The Crimson Light had showed up right on time, thus alleviating not only your distress but also mine. He had saved me from the dark thoughts that had surfaced my mind: Should I leave you behind? Oh, I really don't think I'm good enough. Will I prove myself competent at this phenomenal position? What should I do with him?

Frustration and pain, enmeshed with guilt and shame, had hurt my frontal lobes. With deep and sincere remorse, I knew then to act on my prayers and meditate for a peaceful life. I saw a part of me that I did not like and certainly do not wish to encounter again. My son, I felt certain in that very moment that the Crimson Light had heard me and had answered my prayer. The words of my mouth and the meditation of my heart had been acceptable.

As far as I know, Chatterbox is in respite. We'd learnt to entertain each other over time, and it could be said we now have a good relationship. Chatterbox had always been a faithful and loyal busy-buddy. But there were times that I was so scared that if I had lost him, not only would my life seem no more, but I would have no friends, and the people close to me would think I was dull.

The Crimson Light taught me yet again. I had to find my voice and just imagine dancing to my own new tune, instead of all those tunes that had been labelled for me, like weird, crazy, timid, slut, stupid, skinny, rude, cupped mouth, and so on. As a result, I would continue to dream that one day, I could be free of all labels and stigmas that I did not like because I was beginning to understand I was giving them more attention than necessary. As often said, you get what you place your attention on.

You see, over time, I have cultivated a habit of short but frequent vacations from Chatterbox with the use of prayers, affirmations, and meditations. These vacations are getting increasingly longer because, again, what you give attention to grows.

There were times I felt that Chatterbox was really helpful because he would point out other people in worse conditions than I. In turn, I would feel better about myself, but that illusion would only work for a short while, thus requiring frequent doses of his indulgence and with the potential of addiction. Having done the maths, I know that someone being worse off than me does not actually change the state of my affair, unless I use the observation as a source of inspiration and motivation, so as to dance a different tune.

Conversely, would it seem reasonable that I should feel bad that someone else is presumably better off than I? No doubt this kind of thinking has its place in society but lends its values only to a competitive mentality which we have all been attuned to at some stage. For example, my secret desire for a rich and influential lifestyle did not permit me to use the necessary tools to being successful. I was focused on being better than others. As a result, I drove cars motivated by those who passed me by while I stood waiting for the bus to arrive. Eventually, I drove fancy cars also motivated by other cars that zoomed past me. Then I learnt about engine sizes, speed, and so on. I found out that this state of comparison, imposed by early learning and society as a whole, can render no end in the material world and its superficiality. For there always will be others who exceed your current state. Likewise, there will always be others who will seem to fall short of where you are at. What do you do then? Rejoice?

Finding the right balance was not easy because of dim attitudes which men found too much to handle: too independent or too giving. Women, on the other hand, found me old school and self-righteous, not making financial demands of men. Some even said that I spoiled it for women. What many people didn't know is that I was just learning to find my feet, so that I could dance to my own tune.

I knew that my intention of getting rich was also motivated to prove to others that I could excel beyond their wish for me and show them I can be accepted in the world. This had fostered the worst intention I ever had for men. In my thoughts, I would be in a position that I could have any man I wanted: chew them and spit them out, as my wish for all the hurt they had caused me. I would be rich and make them pay. The Crimson Light, despite my blight, always found a way to express the opposite acts that would teach me to love men, through you, my son. I was unaware that I had been training for my role as the mother of many sons. That is why I believed that I was blessed with a son: to teach me how to appreciate and empathise with men.

Now I am so grateful and thankful that by consenting to the light, I am increasingly developing the art of listening, not only to men but also women. However, while we sing songs that "only women bleed," it is important to strike a balance. Songs like this had also dealt many men an unfair deal. I now believe those men who caused my hurt, at some time in their lives, were hurting too. Somehow, some bled inside whilst another had caused them pain. The biggest disappointment is that it has taken so long to learn this, and that indeed is the sore cry.

Now, though I felt imprisoned and had been given a life sentence, but through desire, the Crimson Light melted the chains through the words of Susan Jeffers: "Feel the fear and do it anyway." I had the faith I would dance with my son again.

It was by listening, son, that I felt your pain, the pain that I sent you away, with the intention to get my business off the ground; the pain of wondering when you would see me again; the pain you were lied to, that you would "see her tomorrow," and tomorrow became a year. It tore me inside. The frequent telephone calls, of course, could not compensate for your ache, and perhaps that is why after a while, you could not be bothered to speak to me over the phone.

It's to comprehend that some people actually take pleasure in hurting another, but it has never been so in your case. I had to consciously permit myself on many occasions to eat or laugh because I would wonder whether you had eaten or felt happy, even though I trusted you were in good care.

Over time, I comforted myself with the idea that at least you got to know your grandparents and other family members, too. I hope that you retained some fond memories of them, including Mr All-Bags-Full, who you got to see a better side of. In turn, your absence also allowed me to discover what you really mean to me and to discover my sense of obligation as a mother.

Our reunion was one of my most joyous and harmonious experiences. The Crimson Light had enveloped us just right. I was also able to help validate my action, not only for the fact that I really felt I acted right, but I had paid attention to the soft voice at three o'clock that morning. In response to the question I had faced, "Why am I here?" I was also presented the bloody combination that unlocked the gate of my imprisoned walls that would unite mother and son once more. That realisation spun the warm glow of optimism, which I followed up by demonstrating an act of faith that I would cope; I would find a way, even without a regular source of income. I had no fear. Just like Harry had paid his loyalty to Mr Altidore;

that's exactly how my friend Frederica had performed the act for you and I to unite; without question, her mission was well accomplished. The Crimson Light had ignited the spark and had set ablaze the love that was hidden so deep inside.

Your little arms around my neck, though nearly five, filled my heart with delight; backpacked with your beaming smiles, it had created a warm glow all around in the atmosphere. There I was on my merry-go-round, because I had consented to the Crimson Light, which whispered, "You are the mother of many sons."

I had my first lesson and my first love. The frequent glances would often mirror back to me, "Oh no, hang on a minute, Mum. Today, I am the teacher and you are the student." Now since I had no clue of the subject matter at hand, I learnt how to take rounds. In hindsight, I found out you were offering me lessons in Actualising Self-full Love. I thank you for a much valued treasure: a mother's consent to the Crimson Light.

Anchoring Points

There are no accidents and no coincidences, but the choices we make:
Today, I am making a choice to see
within,
possibilities, and
treasures.

I am now open and receptive to the guidance of the Crimson Light;
therefore, I am trusting the choice I have made to maintain
courage,
consistency, and
determination.

I rule my mind, which I alone must rule

I have a kingdom I must rule. At times it does not seem I am the Queen (king) at all.

It seems to triumph over me, and tell me what to think, and what to do and feel.

And yet it has been given me to serve whatever purpose I perceive in it.

My mind can only serve.

Today I give its service to the Holy Spirit to employ as He sees fit.

I thus direct my mind, which I alone can rule.

And thus I set it free to do the Will of God [the Crimson Light].

—Helen Schucman, A Course in Miracles

CHAPTER 3

Signpost to the Bridge

The more I thought about the preceding incidences before Mr Barack's Altidore's descent, the more responses I seemed to explore. It was like Deepak Chopra all over in my head: "Why are you here?" and the string of endless answers would flow. One minute, I was like Jack on the beanstalk; the more I climbed, the farther up I got, with seemingly no end, yet I wondered what giant awaited me. Was there someone else to save before I reached the Bridge of Actualising Self-full Love?

The continuous flashbacks of events had penetrated my memory bank once more. Whilst I felt I had actually progressed, with each scenario as a signpost, there was also a sense of wonder; was I there yet? Progression and regression had wedged a picture in my mind that the figure I had seen voluntarily stepping into the tomb casket, just like that, was undeniably a son I had borne. The enveloping sheet of warmth and tenderness conveyed the message that the essence of motherhood is not about perfection or self-incrimination. Rather, it is simply to honour the gift of life granted through the Crimson Light, by which, to love yourself through the act of nurturing your dependent. Therefore, it is important to have faith that you will endure, for your light is sure: a necessary balance to know when to hold on and when to let go. What was I holding on to and needed to let go? I wondered.

With regret streaming down my eyes from the feeling I could no longer hide, a signpost revealed another turning point before I could reach my destination. It painted the picture that I had gotten it wrong, for thinking I was not a good mother. Instead, the only requirement is the true essence of giving and forgiving, of yourself and others; that is what truly matters. A simple exercise of empathy by looking within, and without, is often enough to grant the courage to endure, and "endure you will." That was the message on the main signpost.

Gobsmack with surprise that I had been worthy all along, I ensured to no longer miss a thing, so I carefully gazed at another message that had caused me to sigh: "Remembering your spirit and who you truly are without compromising or apologising is your birthright. However, it is by your self-full expression that you are able to demonstrate unconditional love."

Quite profound, and yet so sweet, the words compelled my head into motion, with reverence. It was whilst raising my head, accompanied by the closing of my mouth, that I discovered I had dribbled onto my bare chest. I was just like a baby without a bib. The Crimson Light had just fed me a delicious dose of unconditional love.

As a mother of many sons, the wetness on my chest reminded me of the fact that

I had taken on the role to give the love that I wanted as a child, but because I had forgotten what it was to be a child, I had to experience that stimuli once more. Even in that instant, I understood that I had been blessed with the assimilation of an emotional dance and that in turn would help me communicate the truth within my heart.

Could I ignore the powerful presence of one who I had borne, who I thought I had lost for good but then felt so near? Once more with Resignation, I humbly paid my vows in acknowledgement of the power of the Crimson Light as I looked at the sign that had led me to my son.

"I choose the feelings I experience, and I decide
Upon the goal I would achieve."

—Helen Schucman, A Course in Miracles

The memories immediately began flooding in. Another sad dance that also meant another sad tune had to be played. Still, I will dance with my son again, I thought.

It felt as though I had woken up, still dazed, in a recovery room, accompanied by voices in my head and faces in my mind.

I had been locked in GPS, as having undergone a major operation. I was to undertake a very important lesson: a course that would awaken the dead that was dormant in me. The woman in black and other strangers said that they had to make a referral for me. This was because my heart was so inflamed and filled with desire to learn how to love unconditionally. All because of my wish of getting onto the Bridge of Actualising Self-full Love.

My bout of extreme joy at the two-page report was a necessary antidote for boosting my immunity. It was the best report I ever had in my entire life, hence the reason why I was determined to find the lost diary in which it was written. You would be so proud of me. Son, the woman in black and the others told me a lot of things.

The embedded secrets had become too heavy to bear; therefore, an incision was necessary, they said. The dead and heavy weight that I had been carrying as though it were a favorite handbag was not conducive to reach my goal: The Bridge of Actualising Self-full Love. Consequently, the Crimson Light had offered me another chance to express gratitude for the kind Pass mark that Mrs Promise had given me in Micoud Secondary School on the island.

Son, I had no idea I was so tired until then. Although they were so good to me, I wish you could have seen for yourself. Oh, they reminded me of my desire to learn how to experience the good in my life, instead of trying too hard, sharing all I have, and often leaving myself without. They said that to continue this way, I would not experience the abundance that the universe has for me. This custom I had to change; otherwise, I could be left not knowing any other way. Son, they told me more things.

It might have been the habit of complaining, but I told them of the burdens that I carried all these years.

They said, "Yes, we know, but by consenting to the Crimson Light, you have made a choice to gently lay the dead down; by that we mean the thoughts and feelings that give no life." They explained to me that it was as though I had been carrying a stillborn child in me. I believe that all this had taken place between the hours of eleven and midnight. I am not sure why, but they referred to it as both "the eleventh hour" and "the watch hour." Somehow, even while I listened, I just couldn't help but think that an everlasting procedure had taken place, since I was replaying the whole event in my subconsciousness.

The woman in black and the others said that for me to live like I always dreamt was attainable, but I had to make my full confession.

I told them, "I have always confessed my sins; even though sometimes the same names were repeated time and time again on my forgiveness list."

Then they made reference to the rich young ruler who asked of Christ, "What must I do to enter the kingdom of heaven?" Christ said unto him, "Go and sell all that you have to the poor." And on hearing this, the young ruler was sad.

Understandably so, for what price can the poor pay for his prized possessions? "My case is different, because I have nothing to sell," I said.

"Just what do you mean? What of your experiences? You bet, they're riches too! The pain that you endured in laying down all, and whatever lessons you have learnt, they are also valued as prized jewels."

They showed me how it could save the poor in spirit and the broken and contrite heart. They also said that I don't always have to go the extra mile, but just ensure to always wear a smile.

The woman in black and the others assured me that although they had lightened my load, by helping me to understand that I was created light, I would need to make a full demonstration of laying my possessions down. When they told me this, like the young ruler, I was sad. My experiences, though enriching, did not seem like prized jewels to me. They explained that my demonstration would, in fact, also be my act of faith and unconditional love: an act of recognising who we truly are. I don't quite know why, but I said it sounded like "buy one get one free." I am not sure what they made of me, but Resignation nudged me as though I had gone insane.

Then I heard "Apart from the choice to decide, nothing is free! And remember, process is process."

I expected Resignation to know what he was talking about, since he is inevitably part of every process.

I suppose this still had to be the best deal I could make to decide to lay the dead weight down. At least I was moving nearer to the Bridge of Actualising Self-full Love. I could not go wrong. In any case, there was still an echo in my ear: "No pain, no gain." Furthermore, the assumption that eventually everyone has to go through this process made me consider myself fortunate that I had indeed approached this particular signpost and would not have the need to be faced with it again.

Now my pain and shame had meaning. All I needed to do was sell my riches to the poor, but that was when I really understood the term "Yard Sale." Now everyone's going to know exactly the sort of stuff I had been keeping inside.

The woman in black and the others saw my dis-ease and said, "This is not just about you; it is also about being of service to others out there. Not only about those that are killing themselves but those who are being killed through shame and pride, just like when you tried to hide. Hence, they are deprived of the free domain of life by which they can make informed choices." They also said that what I was becoming must be witnessed, just like I had witnessed Mr Altidore stepping into the tombed casket, just like that. Then I remembered people like Oprah Winfrey, Iyanla Vanzant, Louise Hay, Denzel Washington, including my friends Stuart Wilde, Paul McKenna and many more who have been of service to others.

The woman in black told me to wear white, but she also reminded me that black or white, we are simply two sides of the same coin. She said that she had worn black to mirror my mourning inside. However, what is most important is to remember that out of the dark comes light. Son, they told me a lot of things.

I told them about you, but it seemed as though they knew you even before I did. That is how they assured me that you were alright, just before I had fallen asleep in GPS, but look! Where are you now? Okay, I suppose my purpose here is to complete my mission and lay my possessions down.

I told them of the mass of my regrets and how I had raised you single-handedly. They also told me that nothing is wasted apart from regrets, which steal away the gift of precious time and energy. And then, as though two familiar voices had rehearsed the response that followed: "When you know better, you do better."

When I heard this, I immediately felt that just had to be the best shortcut to forgiveness. I would use it to save me repeating the same names on my "to forgive" list from there on. That also gave me the confidence to complete my mission of confession. Then, I wouldn't be experiencing hell anymore.

They gave me a long list, like the grid in the Matrix, but I didn't have to go through each one individually. They said, "Just follow three simple rules: Know thyself, Love thyself, and Love thy neighbour as thyself, no more no less." I was so happy for the clarification on that last point. I told them that even as a child, that was what I always tried to do. They laughed and said, "We know, as a child, even in funeral processions, you cried with those who cried, but you were learning about yourself: how to be compassionate, empathic, and sympathetic, and other aspects of love. Now you have a responsibility to look after yourself and deal with your emotions; this you can do by always referring to the seat of your soul, the core of your being where truth lies." Then, they showed me a half-filled cup, and I knew straight away what I should do.

I had completed my refresher's course on Faith because I was half-filled.

The burning feelings and sensations had pivoted my attention

To the signpost, that would help me complete my mission of confession.

Son, this you must believe: that I love you with my whole being. Forgive me, I did you wrong. Yes, I know I did you wrong! So many things I ought to have said. I know there were times you felt very sad not having your father around. I know you felt I was responsible for your father's absence, and in the past, I felt that way too. But after all these years, I haven't been able to come up with any better solution. Son, I am sorry. I am sorry I did not know what I had done, by not telling the truth about your father and me.

How do I begin to tell you what I thought you couldn't bear?

Please understand. How could I have simply told you, without a voice of my own, that your father was a drug baron and a fraud?

Where could I have found the courage to let you know that he didn't care for either you or me? You don't know this, but he had been sentenced to many years for masterminding a big scam. Son, I never had the courage to tell you that. I do understand why you were often very angry, even though I was often at the hot end of your pain. Oh, how I wish I told you every time I was nudged by Resignation through the Crimson Light. Instead, I simply and painfully concealed inside what you should have known. How can I reach you in that tomb below and tell you what you must know? How can I? How can I? Tell me, how can I? The only thing I know for sure is, now that I have consented to the light and observed the signpost, I must complete my mission.

I could have told you, son, so many times when the Crimson Light had shone through. All I had to do was trust that you'd be alright. I guess I demonstrated a strong belief that you could not handle such a loss. It's just that each time I tried to tell you and tested the waters, so to speak, by sharing some light childhood experiences, you seemed unable to take it in. Take, for instance, carrying bananas and pumpkin and ginger on my head; even that you couldn't fathom. By this I hope you understand the plight had stricken and paralysed my ability to explain what was burning way down in me. What was I to do with all my dirty secrets, especially those I found hard to bear? Even now, I question what I ought to say and not say, but the faithful Crimson Light reminded me, "No more lies to bear."

My beloved son, please hear what I have to say; although you're in that tomb, I came here just for you. I thought I could hide forever, but the Crimson Light embodied me with a heat that was almost unbearable. What I didn't know, then, is that each time I resisted the nudge of Resignation, to tell you the truth, the more benumbed or insane I became. Subsequently, my arteries got tighter, as I would release myself in the daily dose of three glasses of wine. Son, I haven't forgotten that to lay all the weight is indeed the mission I must complete.

Each time I encountered a torturing experience, it felt as if the heat of the Crimson Light had become hotter. Now, I understand why it was so: because the constant consumption of alcohol near the heat would quickly ignite into flames. Thus, I would be left feeling severely scorched by the signpost I failed to obey.

There were times the light shone so bright that its heat would just slay my soul to rest, and that's what I think I had gone through that watchful hour in GPS. On recovering such an experience, one is bound to be sore. That is why, sometimes, I'd masked myself in lovely protective clothes, which I made, as you already know. I would cover the evidence that I had indeed been hiding something shameful that had caused the hurt. I'd quickly patch them up, at the slightest sign of a rip, because no one needs to know. I cloaked myself in matching shoes and handbags, not to ask about makeup. I had every shade to wear. I masked in my smiles, and of course, that I did well. I probably wore every hairstyle of various shades and even invented my own, too. Basically, I was concerned with "hair today" and it'd be "gone tomorrow." That is why it was often said that I was a bit of a stoosh. But honestly, that's how I learnt to survive and hold myself in high esteem. Either way, I could not hide what I truly felt inside.

I found myself feeling excruciating pain, till my body cried and said, "No more; this is insane!" The migraine attacks extended and darted all the way down my spine, nearly crippling all mobility. I bawled out, "No more lies! No more secrets for this heart to bear."

Then I embarked upon a psalm; the Crimson Light had shined in my despair. There I took comfort as I repeated the words:

"Wherever can I go from thy presence? If I should go to the outmost parts of the sea you are there."

And I now truly embrace the faithful force of the Crimson Light, which I believe has always been with me and you, too.

Son, I don't know how I could have thought that it was okay to hide behind those wretched sins. On the other hand, how could I have simply told you what I did not find the guts to do? Well, as you might have guessed by now, I did pretty well by masking the truth, the truth about my life, such as why you never had a brother or a sister; that I really do not know for sure. Long before I even met your father, I miscarried and went on to abort not one but two pregnancies, a shame that validated the labels handed to me in my youth. Son, please forgive me. I confess. I did what I thought was best.

I know you always thought I was bright, but as it turned out, I often felt blight even in my pursuit to see the light. Well, I suppose my frequent tendency of seeking the Crimson Light of Actualising Self-full Love had indeed helped me to shift my focus in various ways. As you know, for that reason, we attended church, in addition to the therapeutic interventions I underwent, with the intention just to learn the pathway to the Crimson Light.

I often felt that I paid attention to the light, but that was often through a plight that would in turn remind me of the importance of observe the signposts. Consequently, I realised that I was being slowly transformed and was being led nearer to the Actualising Self-full Love. The process, however, at times glimmered and would seethe from my awareness, so I could hardly tell for sure exactly what worked well and what didn't. Consequently, I would lose all control by allowing a man to hold my hand, a gesture I thought would lead in arm's way, but instead I'd often end up in harm's way. That was exactly how I ended up marrying your father, by doing my dumbest to avoid despair.

I was trying very hard not to repeat the mistake that my mother had done: another me, born of a different father to my siblings. "I would only have my child to the man who is going to be my husband" was a sentiment that had been entrenched in my bones.

Now, since your father proposed before we did it, as a real gentleman I considered him to be, he was certainly the one for me.

Two months before you came inside my belly, your father, an intelligent, stylish, and very charismatic gentleman, asked me to marry him. You probably have some idea from that picture I know you secretly hold dear. Sensing that we had a lot in common, I considered his proposal.

"Yes, I will marry you," I said.

A few weeks later, off to bed we geared. Oh, what a joy we shared. He boasted about the fact that he'd actually impregnated me on his "first shot," as he called it, and I too was joyously impressed. Strangely enough, my mother told me that's how I came into being too: at their first (but it was also her and my father's only) shot.

However, that was enough to open the flood-gate of all my fears, to not be fertile like Mother. Yet, with the adverse reactions of various contraceptives to my body, I also wondered, like Mother, whether contraceptives were a good thing at all. The convergence of thoughts and attitudes was too near to what I was actually trying to avoid. For instance, Mother had gotten pregnant with me whilst her husband was in the UK. That made me wonder whether my husband would also go away.

If that were to be the case, perhaps, like Mother, I would attempt an abortion and end having a baby stubbornly anchored inside my womb, like I was to her womb. Perhaps I would have to rely on the pendulum for the answer to the burning question that Mother felt stricken by: "Will he still have me if I tell the truth that I got pregnant by another man?" The pendulum swung Yes for Mother. By then, I was two months in her belly when your grandma was rushed to the UK in a hurry.

The shame and embarrassment had caused me to grow lonely inside; throughout the situation, I tried, perhaps too hard, to avoid the shame.

You were only two months inside me when your father began forming the fool.

Can I tell you, son, that I really did not know how to own up this truth and to tell you outright that I, too, had my share of faults, and by that, I did your dad a dirty? I stood him up at the registry office, including the guests, too. And that, I am telling you, was with malicious intention, for the wrong I felt he had done. I'm really not so proud about it anymore. Please allow me to give you the picture.

We agreed he'd moved in with me very soon after the proposal so that we could save some money for the wedding. It happened that with just days to go before the big day, your father disappeared. I even feared he was dead. You can imagine, I was extremely worried. Moreover, he had not come forth to pay his share of the expenses. Subsequently, everything was left down to me. In addition, I was also new at running my clothing business and juggling life the best I could.

It was the second evening of his disappearing act. I felt strangely suspicious as I sat on the bed, all alone, wondering what to do. After a moment of stillness, I could clearly hear the words repeated in my head, until I blurted them right out: "Something's not right! Something's definitely not right!"

Immediately, I felt shivers all over my body as I gazed at a small suitcase, which was on top of the wardrobe directly in front of me.

Then I heard, "There is something in that suitcase that you should see."

Then I repeated, "There is something in that suitcase that I should see!"

I was scared because I was not in the habit of prying into someone's personal belongings. However, I believed in my heart that the message was true. I was becoming acquainted with the voice of the Crimson Light, which never lies.

Following a deep breath, I prayed, "Lord, I ask that you protect and forgive me for what I am about to do."

I got down the suitcase, but it was digitally locked. I took another deep breath and lifted my head to the heavens, and without shifting the dials, I made another prayer:

"Lord, I believe there is something in that case I should see, and if this is so, let it be that I should see what's inside. And please give me the strength to handle whatever is in there."

I then slid both of my thumbs up and down, simultaneously, onto the rows of numbers on either sides of the locks, and it clicked! Viola! I had opened the case. Even then, I had no doubt that I had been guided by the Crimson Light.

Son, you may find it difficult to believe, but what I am telling you are true things I saw that day. Unbelievable, but nonetheless true. I felt so disturbed and upset to my stomach, like my emotions had instantly been hijacked; I spent what seemed like hours on the "throne." I just needed a small place to hide. Son, how could I have told you this? I didn't want to believe what I had seen, that day. I wanted to believe a lie, that it wasn't so. I felt so stupid. Stupid, that I agreed to marry your father. Stupid, I had spent all my money on the wedding plans; the invitations were already sent out. Who is this man? I asked myself. He had seven different passports, as though one for each day of the week (or was he creating a new world order?). Each passport showed a different name, different date of birth, and different place of birth, but all with his face. Son, it was a very frightening experience. A million times, I asked myself, How am I going to deal with this? As much as I did not want my child to ever be raised without his father or to do it on my own, those were the options that squared me in the eyes.

My life's dread had come upon me. To be brought up by both parents was my wish for you, and that was very important to me.

Your father knew this. I had not learnt to dwell on what I wanted; instead, I spent several years dreading this eventuality: ours would not be a nuclear family.

Son, what I want to say is not easy, but I will explain so that I can complete my mission. Besides his own, your father had approximately twenty new passports, including some with other faces. They were British and Dutch, German, and those of the United States of America.

As to who your father is, I can only tell you what he told me: that he was Nigerian, and his mother was from Cameroon. Now, I was inclined to believe that this was true, and credit to him that he had an accent that supported this story. Apart from that, I am not sure about the place or date of birth, or anything else he claimed to be real about him. Going by the uncertainty that I carried over the years, I am guessing you must have felt quite lost, and perhaps that was the cause of you stepping in the smoky black hole, just like that.

Son, bear with me while I catch my breath, because there's more.

You wouldn't believe: that suitcase contained a very large stack of birth and death certificates; according to Chatterbox, that was deadly scary. Undoubtedly, that had elicited a dreadful feeling inside me. In addition, there were two albums which I had previously flicked through. There he was, your dad, lovingly embracing two young boys, who he had managed to convince me were his cousin's children. It transpires that I was able to make sense of his behaviour of pulling the album away from me. Son, I know you are my one and only child, but I really believe that you have at least two brothers somewhere out there in London.

You may find this hard to believe, but there's more. In the case were also countless chequebooks from various bank accounts and from different countries. On top of all that, I discovered a woman's naked picture neatly placed between my folded bed sheets. Then

I understood this to mean the signature on the signpost that said "Do something," followed another one that read "No entry for good thoughts until further notice!" So I did the dirty.

I cooked up a plan and called my friends, Mo and Dot. I had them swear to support my plan of action. Son, I was hurt. Moreover, I felt tired of feeling treated like dirt. Trust me, this was the best I could do at the time. Eventually, your father showed up two days before we were meant to say, "I do," as though all was well. He just could not see what the fuss was about, that I was concerned about his whereabouts. His response was, I was overreacting. Wishing he would attempt to make it right by me, I said, "Okay, perhaps you're right." I had all the ingredients for making a most memorable impact on him: shame, pride, ignorance, and embarrassment, including determination that seldom fails me.

On the day deemed most memorable for both of us, your father showed up about one o'clock in the morning. I pretended to be asleep, but needless to say, I could hardly wait for the break of day to execute my plan. I pretended all was well. We went to the reception hall, to ensure that everything was in place. As a matter of fact, we worked very well together. "Make sure to get there on time," I said to him as we kissed goodbye. It was back at the apartment for him and off to my friend's home for me.

To ensure that I was going to stick to my plan, I didn't even finish the dress, nor did I take it with me, just in case I got tempted into feeling sorry for him. As it turned out, I nearly did.

A Rolls-Royce pulled up outside the apartment, a rarity for an area with a tarnished reputation of poverty and crime. The neighbours, and in particular the children, were eagerly looking to see who was going to be riding in the prestigious carriage. My hair was not styled as you'd expect to see a bride's. The only thing that resembled a wedding was the white T-shirt worn over my jeans. I was able to convince the driver, who was ever so smartly dressed, that he indeed had the wrong address. Son, I wish I could end right here, but it just didn't happen that way. The Rolls-Royce returned to ensure that he hadn't made the mistake of going to the wrong address. Again he was sent back with the same response as before.

It was about three o' clock that afternoon, and I was thinking, All that wonderful seafood, perfect aphrodisiacs, cocktails, and fine champagne, plus that lovely cake, just sitting on the table, and I am here, hungry like hell. Son, I hate to tell you this, but the driver came back a third time, but this time, he brought Auntie Lorraine. Once upstairs, Lorraine knew that they indeed had the right address. She said that this was the last chance because they had saved the last slot for us; that was, if I changed my mind. Lorraine had never ceased her loyalty towards me.

By that time, I think I'd gone a bit cuckoo in the head. You see, the process had taken much longer than I had anticipated. In hindsight, I can only imagine that it must have been Chatterbox and Resignation in competition, seeking my attention to express their views on the matter. Yes! I had definitely brushed shoulders with insanity then, because I was laughing and crying all at the same time.

The look in Lorraine's eyes and the tone of her voice conveyed a sadness as she said, "Sis, I don't know whether you are laughing or crying, so I don't know what to say."

My emotions seemed so interwoven; I could hardly tell them apart, so I had nothing that could lend her peace in that moment. "Anyway, it's not as though I have ceased to exist; him treating me like that, I will not change my mind," I exclaimed in my defence.

Later, that evening, I was told that a fight had been broken out over the foods and drinks because the supposed groom's friends retaliated by claiming all the goods from the hall. My brothers knew otherwise, that the only thing Euyah had paid for was the

Rolls-Royce, so they insisted that the friends leave empty-handed. That night, your father, Euyah (one of his many aliases), met up with me back at my apartment and asked me, "Why didn't you show up?"

I gently said that I thought things through and it just didn't feel right. That's why I change my mind.

"You could have told me," he said. "Just to let you know, I am not perturbed."

Later, I checked out the meaning of "perturb" and thought, Really?

My family and friends ensured my safety by offering to stay with me that night and changed the lock to the front door. In hindsight, it was a necessary contingency. I had not even given thought to the idea I may come to harm; perhaps it's because I still felt the presence of the Crimson Light. Your father no doubt was a cool-headed guy; his friends, on the other hand, if they had the chance, they would eat me for supper. I was told that they were really mad at me. Although this ugly thing had happened, the following day I was back at work, doing what I did best: making garments. Of course, I had also furnished everyone's table with the topic (unbelievable):

For this, I must catch my breath, because there is more.
Even you would need to catch your breath;
That was if you could still hear what I have to tell you.

What I am about to tell you is not easy at all. Son, this is where I felt really, really stupid and embarrassed. Your father maintained contact, as he obviously seemed excited about you.

One day, he offered to take me out to the pictures, with my big belly, to see Terminator. Afterwards, I thought that was not healthy at all. I had learnt that it's good to be happy and singing to your baby while they're in the womb, and I took this seriously, and Terminator was not fun to me. Apart from that, you were happy; I would not allow anything to disturb our peace.

The time had come, and I was going to be given a Caesarean section because you were bridged in my tummy. The doctor had hoped you would turn around, but being your mother's child, you stayed put. Your father maintained that he could not be with us due to an employment training course. But I was blessed to have Auntie Maggie and my friend Fina to support me.

Auntie Maggie was certainly one of the nicest people I had ever known. Even though a lot younger than myself, when it came to you, she seemed far better prepared than I was. I was a bit of a workaholic, busy meeting deadlines, whilst she was a shopper-holic, standing on lines shopping for you. She passed at the tender age of forty to cancer; many of the secrets we shared went untold to those who should have heard them. That is why I am now telling you what I believe you ought to have known. However, instead of the eight o'clock appointment the next morning, you decided to enter into this world on your own timing. As often said, you really had a mind of your own. I didn't agree with the pangs and pulling of my heart strings, and including the strain at the base of my spine, but over time, I admired your tendency to stand your ground.

We went back home, and I went back to work; still, you have always been my pride and joy, yes, including my hurt too. I had gotten over the reality of not having your father around, and it seemed like just as we were settling into our mother-and-son relationship, he was back in our lives.

Euyah spoke as if having a son was an honour in his speech, but I can't say that he was financially supportive. Yes, he did buy you a tricycle for your first birthday, and I must say, he seemed to absolutely enjoy holding you, and he always seemed affectionate. But when you were six months old, your father showed up with a mature-looking woman he called Auntie. She wore a white veil that reminded me of the women who would place a scarf on their head in no particular order, to receive Holy Communion at Sunday Mass.

She told me, "The child should have his father around, especially a boy child," and they promised that they would be very supportive of us. That day, your father seemed unnaturally affectionate towards me, using tactics as if from a textbook. It was clear that he had been influenced by the woman with the white veil. On confronting my suspicion, as he led me to the bedroom, that followed her gesture of a hand wave (as is saying go on) he admitted that he had been drilled by her. But when I questioned him about the photograph of the naked woman that I had found between the folded bed sheets, he totally denied it, including what I had seen in the case that day; he had no idea what I was talking about.

Well, son, here is what I really want to say: A few weeks later, your father and I were back at the same registry office at Hackney Town Hall, in East London, ordering another marriage license (this time, he gave yet another birth date). I remember asking myself, What am I doing here? How did I get myself here again?

Son, I honestly believe that I had gotten hooked by the lovely green scarf presented by the woman with the white veil. The following month, I said, "I do," to your father. It was a small wedding. However, I decided to enjoy the idea that you were physically there to attend. After that day, I never saw the white-veiled juju woman again who he claimed to be is Aunt.

Shortly after we got married, Euyah handed me all sorts of papers to sign, as though all I knew was how to write my name. I promised to go through them later, but later proved too late, or no longer necessary.

One morning, your father asked me to accompany him on a short trip to Holborn, but without explaining why. He took me to a lawyer's office down Chancery Lane, where I discovered he had a deportation case pending. Unknown to me until that point, I held the ace card. As your mother, I could request to have my child's father given permission to stay in the country and fulfill his obligation to us. The marriage was clearly one of convenience, so I asked for time to think things through. Sad as I was to think that I had been used, that night, I went into the core of my heart. It was there I embarked on that signpost once more: "No entry for good thoughts until further notice." I hid myself in the bosom of the Crimson Light as I knelt against the bed and pondered an idea a friend had given me: I should put some salt in Euyah's shoes; that would send him packing. My timidity would not allow me to do so. Plus, I was also scared that he'd find out and hurt me.

Then I heard a voice whisper, "Pray and believe with your whole heart that God will help you."

So I prayed:

"Dear God, Lord and Saviour, help me out of this mess.
I believe something strange has happened.
But you are God; you can do this, get this man out of my life for good,
Even if it means coping on my own. You'll be there for us anyway."

About three days later, Euyah showed up at my apartment, from another training course. I asked him to take his ready-packed stuff out of my home, but he just arrogantly laughed in my face and said he had nowhere else to put them. Well, he'd quickly found somewhere by the time he got to the bottom of the stairs: I found the strength and threw the suitcase onto the ground, all the way from the second floor (making sure not to hurt anyone, of course). You should've seen how quickly he made the U-turn.

Son, a man should really treat his partner with respect and hold her in high esteem. It's important to remember his behaviour in the relationship is an investment in not just her but himself. While she is the reciprocator, he had better ensure that his deposits are good, because most women are capable of making a meal out of anything. Do all you can to ensure it's a delicious one.

I also learned God certainly answers prayers, but you must be willing to exercise mental and, in some cases, physical fitness too. However, I did not anticipate the need for a stronger dose of mental stamina for what was to follow.

Now you know I told you about the drug thing? I wish I didn't have to tell you, really. Nevertheless, I want you to hear this. Approximately nine months after you were in St Lucia, I was indoors on my own one night; it was the watch hour. I heard someone trying to break down the front door. In my defence, I grabbed an empty bottle, intending to wallop the potential intruder over the head. However, being averse to violence, I thought I would present him a chance to assess his situation, so I asked, "Who is it? What do you want?"

It turned out that it was the police. They told me to open the door immediately, which I did. They'd caught your father with drugs, and according to them, he gave them my address as his. They ransacked my home. That was so humiliating. They even chucked my bedside friend onto the floor, as though that was nothing. I was treated with no dignity whatsoever.

One of them said, "Come on, tell us where it is."

"Tell you where what is?" I replied.

"Even if it's just one spliff, we won't do you anything."

If you won't do me anything, I thought to myself, why bother asking for one spliff? But I did not mess with marijuana. Yes, I experimented with it and decided that was definitely not for me. Come to think of it, the cops could have set me up too, so they weren't so bad, after all.

Anyway, the next day, I received a phone call from your father's solicitor, requesting that I bring him some stuff. My initial reaction was to be supportive, but I decided to sleep on the idea, just like I did in GPS. I think that is what the watch hour means: to sleep on an idea. Things become much clearer the next day. It appeared that your father did not care if I got locked up and risked having no one to look after you.

I showed up in the gallery at Holloway Magistrate Court to hear for myself as they read the charges against him. That was when I knew the extent of the mess that he'd got into and the lucky escape I had made. The allegations against him seemed to answer many of my questions regarding his frequent absences. I was also faced with the sadness that you may never really get to know your father. I do not recall what name he was charged under, but the officers read out a long list of aliases. I can only assume that they put all the names into a bag and had a lucky dip so as to ascertain what name they would call him.

The prosecutors claimed that he had purchased several houses using the names of different people who were no longer alive. He was also believed to be the ringleader of supplying false passports to immigration agencies in various parts of the world. In addition, it was reported that he had been caught red handed with approximately ten kilos of cocaine, and that was not including what he and his friends had flushed down the toilet.

I thought, Serves you right, while you live the high life and not even providing for your child! Right there and then, I pronounced him guilty as charged.

Regardless of the poor choice I had made, the Crimson Light had not ceased to shine on me. There was always a signpost directing my path. I could've been arrested along with him and his so-called cousin and his cousin's wife (who thought women should only live by expensive shoes and matching handbags). In hindsight, I realised that it was their way of trying to entice me into their ring, since she felt the need to boast about paying hundreds of pounds for a pair of shoes.

However, my training on Mr All-Bags Full's farm had prepared me to value hard work as the means to achieving what I wanted. Perhaps the salt in the shoes really did have its place in such a case, after all. Again, the Crimson Light reminded me that we are all on this journey to becoming; regrets are a total waste of the gift of time.

My mission to lay all down now seemed complete, but I was still learning. I learned that even the things we regret can in themselves serve us as the bedrock to finding our true purpose in life. I certainly would not have had you as my son; you would not have existed otherwise. The same goes for every seemingly insignificant decision that we make. They present to us the lessons to make sense of our world: They could be young, old, male, female, creatures, trees and plants, the firmament, the ocean, the sun, the moon and stars, a stone, music, and so on; they're all teachers. That is why we ought to remember that we are always in a classroom; just as I was in GPS. All we have to do is follow the signpost to actualise love, which is often nearer than breath.

Son, it became very clear that the power of the Crimson Light, though smitten by its brightness, had showed me why I was there. The woman in black and the others helped me to develop my capacity to draw on my life's experiences. Like "Jack and the Beanstalk," the more I climbed, the more I was able to see the beauty of the Crimson Light in each experience and on the various signposts. I was able to stand even stronger than before. That is why I was also able to stand in witness to seeing my son, Mr Altidore, stepping into the tombed casket, just like that, thus presenting before me another signpost that I would follow.

Anchoring Points

There are no accidents and no coincidences, but the choices we make;
today, I am making a choice to embrace
people,
plants, and
places.

I am now open and receptive to the guidance of the Crimson Light;
therefore, I am trusting the choice I made to
feel,
reflect, and
accept.

Gnashes of pain crying at my heart's door: "Let me out! Let me out!"
Why at this moment, so unexpected, do you scream at me?
What is the grave deed of offense that rattles the locks and bolts of your years?
Why do you choose such moments of inconvenience?
Is it just to drive me insane?

Often racing to get my attention,
While I endeavour to ease myself into stillness,
As gazing at a flower,
Then, suddenly, I'd hear "Let me out! Let me out!"

I seem to have mistaken you for intense joy.
Is it simply because I have used you to mask my face?
How do I now know which one you are, joy or pain?
I suppose, I will know for sure only when I let you out.

Pain at my door, I tried to hush you inside,
Whilst walking down the street,
Yet you scream, "Let me out! Let me out!"
Sometimes I tend to give in, but then, someone passes by,
And I am left with the need to share a smile,
At which time, I am compelled to say, "Can you just wait a little while?"

Pain at my door, louder and louder, a noise I am too weary to bear.
Are you my friend? Are you my foe? Which one should I hold?
Pain at my heart's door, I know you are there,
But must you show up and let the whole world know
How long I have kept you in here?

Should I have been so accommodating
To let you remain here after so many years?
Now, I see, that the contract did not make it clear:
Which specific year?
Pain at my door, or whichever one you are,
Joy or pain, I will know for sure, as I open my heart's door.
I now declare your full permission to roll down through my tears.

CHAPTER 4

Your Boarding Pass to the Bridge

It's strange how we can remember all about the years, months, and weeks that have gone by, but not yesterday. Something so extraordinary had passed you by that you don't quite know how to forgive yourself for missing it. That's how it seemed for me. It had been the first hour of the new era, just before seeing Mr Barack Altidore step into the tombed casket, just like that. The scene had been the stimuli taking me down memory lane once more, with many sublanes necessary for my destination to getting onto the Bridge of Actualising Self-full Love.

I was up again like before, and it was eleven minutes past eleven (11.11 a.m.); four ones had registered in my mind. For some unknown reason, I saw a lot in that eleventh hour. Still, something strange was happening. This was not sleep. This was different and seemed longer than the one in GPS, where I was led by Mrs Blanchard's lookalike, the woman in black. The difference was waking in my bed and assuring myself, with a sense of relief as well as an element of surprise, "I am alive! I am alive."

Eleven days into my forty-day ritual, I didn't bother to seek for validation anymore. As to why? I was now in the flow. It was an idea that had popped in my head after my rereading of the book of St

Matthew from the Holy Bible. Jesus Christ had prayed and fasted in the desert, for forty days and forty nights. I felt like I had been in a desert anyway; I was seeking to connect with my spirit.

The inclination to find my spirit guide through a meditation on YouTube had sparked an inner dialogue, with little concern about which of my separate selves had spoken: "I think my guide's name is Matthew." Then, I asked myself about other Matthews that I knew. There were just two, my former schoolmates on the island of St Lucia. I liked them both, though it often troubled my heart how others treated the one who wore braces on his legs. Matthew felt right, especially for the fact that I was drawn to the book again after a year or so of its absence.

Followed by an uninterruptable sense of commitment, I wrote a short plan of action which stated my oath for my sustenance in the wilderness. I marked out my dates and placed my attention on what was to be my ritual for forty days, which was in direct contrast to the colourful events that were programmed on the children's calendar. As the law of attraction would have it, all my needs and desires were met before I even asked. I just had taken home the calendar on which I indicated the dates. This was my affirmation; it helped me to acknowledge that I had all the resources necessary, including water, a towel, and oils, and I had time for my ritual.

Use a few drops of nine different aura-cleansing essential oils once each morning for forty days, and meditate morning and evening. In addition, I would be mindful of my thoughts and never fail to express gratitude. That had been my prescription, after which I would have acquired a better way of living.

"Today's dose administered later than usual; the clock shows eleven o'clock sharp," I said, just as I had observed the clock on the wall in GPS. Pain like daggers pierced my back and my sides had left me feeling as though each individual rib had no tissue holding them together and could suddenly give way.

I did my best with every deep breath, with my mind-force mentally distributing as much oxygen as possible through my lungs. As a form of guarantee and for sustainability, I imagined giving each rib a double dose of air required and the same to every cell in my body. I will be fine, I will be fine, I tried to assure myself.

The lingering pain beckoned me to shout out to my niece for help. Just a hand passing over my back would soothe me, at least to ease some of the pain, I thought, yet I failed to obey my body's simple request. I longed for someone's hand to soothe my torso because that's where all the pain was stored. Even the weight of my breasts seemed too much to bear; I lifted them up. From there on, with Resignation, I consented to abide by the demands and guidance of the Crimson Light's fleeting rays in my head, and that was despite the blight of intense pain.

So the pain in my back as never before have I experienced such a thing. Courageously, I walked my way downstairs to the oil cabinet, and as I poured every drop into the white square basin, I would say, "God, I thank you for this." I reminded myself that I had no idea how much any of the oils (which were of good quality) had cost. Up the stairs, I said, "I love myself; therefore, I am taking care of myself. But what did Louise Hay say about back pain again? This is not the lower back, like I had a few times, worrying about finance. This is serious! It is my top and middle back."

A dialogue was unreservedly taking place amongst my separate selves. As usual, I topped up the basin with hot water and placed it near the door, whilst allowing the sweet aroma to permeate my senses.

I felt a slight sense of rush. Chatterbox was in my head: "Hurry, hurry! Get under the shower."

Resignation's tone synchronised with my pace: "Remember, it never makes sense to hurry or worry."

So I took my time.

"Breathe in deeply and now exhale fully." It was the voice of Rick Clarke in my head. I continued to push the air through each rib. I stepped into the shower-room with the water already gushing down, a notch hotter than usual: just hot enough to bear.

I first aligned my most painful area to the mass of the pressure gushing down. Water so good, I said to myself.

Now Resignation had just confirmed that this was probably going to be the longest shower I would ever have, so I resigned, gently swerving from side to side, whilst I continued with deep breaths. I had to ensure I consoled every inch of my back, from the top of my neck down to the base of my spine, with mental assurance. Whilst pulling the air in deeply, I had taken intervals of looking at my back and soothing it with my eyes, still aiming for an even distribution inside. It felt like each rib was crying out for its own individual attention, like a baby busily turning its face for the nipple.

I cried out, for the blades of pain had penetrated the very core of my being. Resignation had effortlessly taken control. From side to side, I continued to sway, attending to each nerve that'd been touched by the daggers. A thought crossed my mind: I wish that the power of the shower was stronger, but I quickly realised that Chatterbox was still active, so I resorted to immerse in whatever I had because I knew then that I had everything I possibly needed in that moment. So intermittently, I anchored onto the memory of the solace I felt under the island's Latille Waterfalls, pounding all over my body. The bliss I relived in that moment caused me to smile. Then I resigned to the Crimson Light. I dedicated the moment to endure whatever pain and accept whatever change that day in my ritual was presenting.

I struggled to pray, as the words only seemed to surface through the habit I had cultivated. The absence of utterances seemed to lack the cohesion to even express what I felt or desired. However, I comforted myself with the belief that God was still hearing or feeling my heart.

My rituals were usually bathed in affirmative statements for healing my body and mind:

> I love and I am loved; therefore, I am loving.
> I am joy and I am joyous; therefore, I am joyful.
> I am gracious and I am graceful.
> I am freedom and I am free.
> I am peace and I am peaceful.
> I am creative and therefore I create.
> I am prosperous.
> I am of divine intelligence, therefore I am …

I had some resistance with acknowledging my intelligence, so I increased the numbers of repetition and would end by saying "All is well in my world." Most of the words and sentiments were now replaced in my mind with "Divine spirit guides me, leads me, and nurtures me."

A lovely poem by Emmet Fox had conveniently resurfaced in my mind: God is the only presence and the only power. God, you are fully present with me now, I told myself.

"No lathering your body today. You've been under the shower for a while now," Chatterbox said, getting a little over his head.

"Just observe the Crimson Light, and remember your desire for actualising self-full love," said Resignation.

My two friends seemed to be in competition for leadership. Resignation had won, whilst Chatterbox just quieted himself down, with his tongue on his tail.

Now, it was just water and I, delving into a total new dimension. I was operating in submission to the bridge, through the Crimson

Light: My dream was live. The awareness of oneness somehow, for a short moment, had still generated a degree of fear, but Resignation's alertness and presence had made this seem a passing phase.

"Now suppose they open all the cold taps downstairs and cause an uneven distribution in the water temperature; you could get scalded, you know. Remember, that's how your cousin Erick's wife ended up getting severely scald." I think that was Chatterbox carrying on.

"Yeah," I said, "I have seen that happen in a movie, too. I often wondered about how she managed to get so severely scalded under the shower. Perhaps she was feeling like I am right now and was too tired to think clearly. She might have wanted to close the tap but ended up turning it in the opposite direction. That's how I think she had hot water gushing all over her body; maybe she made it worse by panicking."

Then I immediately remembered to be mindful of what I was entertaining because according to Sonia Couchette, the word "wonder" usually sends out a strong message to the subconscious mind. Therefore, I hoped that my "wondering" would not be experientially answered, thus getting more than I had bargained for.

Chatterbox continued telling me that I should be mindful of how much water that I was using; maybe I was being monitored so the bill payer would not think that I was being inconsiderate. Then, I made a conscious effort, as though using up every breath I had left, to respond, "I, Lauviah, now give myself total permission to stay under this shower for as long as I wish. And I deserve it. I am now actualising self-full love."

With Resignation and feeling lethargic, I ignored the different guises of intonations of Chatterbox's prompts for my attention. It was important to remain focused. I knew that something extraordinary was happening. Moreover, I did not know what it was, apart from the fact that all I really wanted, in that moment, was to just ease the staggering pain in my back.

This time, I felt gratitude for the small shower space that previously seemed restricting; it was now supporting my body in a standing position. Though standing at an angle, as I rested my head onto the wall, my only concern was to avoid collapsing onto the floor. It's often been said that water is life, and I believe this to be true too, so I imagined that each cell in my body was being submerged, with the feeling of water all around it.

Every now and then, I could hear myself drift into dark thoughts: What if I collapse like Richard, who experienced his first attack of myasthenia gravis [a disease of extreme muscle weakness] under the shower? Sporadically, I would absorb the beauty of the Crimson Light, which assured me of its presence with Resignation; then I would whisper, "Spirit, guide me."

The repetition had become more frequent when, the next thing I knew, I heard a sweet song from Louise Hay's Affirmations playing on YouTube. It played gently in my head: "I am so blessed, I am so glad, I am so glad, I am so grateful for all that I have."

I don't know whether I got all the words right, but it resonated with me, especially then. I had previously made a conscious effort to ensure the reverberation would replace the constant "I'm the Map! I'm the Map! I'm the Map" from Dora the Explorer, the children's television programme. My grandnephew Zachiah had driven everyone in the household almost insane with the nonstop repetition of the same episode. Although we all were tired of it and hated it, nevertheless, we all got caught up, singing along to this tune: "I'm the Map."

Now the crux of the ritual was the pouring of oiled-water over me. With an alert enough mind, ensuring not to burn myself, I turned off the tap and reached out for the basin. Not surprisingly, the water had turned cold, so I topped it up with the use of my overhead cup: a plastic container which I had taken from the kitchen downstairs. In my opinion, it should have been out of the house but now it was further in, upstairs. Chatterbox reminded me once more that I was too stoosh for that thing and that I should use a classier item to bathe myself, especially if I claimed to be about loving myself.

My response was the same as before: "I am now choosing to think about its use, and not its look."

I felt like I had had a deep tissue massage. Normally, I would pray over my basin of oiled-water: "I am thankful for this water; let my life be as sweet as these fragrancies, and may the water heal me, and let my life so shine before men that they would come to know the sweetness of the Crimson Light." I often imagined being surrounded by angels as witnesses; whatever was said, it was so.

However, this time, there was no praying (well, at least not in the usual way). For each scoop of water over my head, I'd take a deep breath and just say, "Spirit, heal me. Spirit guide me. Oh, God, I thank you!" Then a question popped into my head: "But why?" Then I said, "God, I want to thank you," and then I heard "What for?"

By then, my only wish was not to collapse, but Resignation gently whispered, "You will not be given more than you can bear."

I thought, Okay, I know that is supposed to make me feel better, but this kind of sentiment never made much sense to me, because people die of not being able to bear anymore. What happens then? Oh, I get it! God stops giving them …

But would that not mean that God is responsible for all human pain? Too much to think about, I concluded.

I finished performing my sacred ritual, and on exit from the shower, I realised I had not wrapped myself up, so I hastened my pace to avoid the chance of being spotted by my curious nephew Sam, who the previous day had tried to see my naked bottom. I barely made it to my room, only four feet or so away, but I felt like I had been on a long and exhausting journey.

Still very wet, I just wanted to collapse in bed and never mind the drench. Then again, perhaps I would feel better to write, just to ease the pain, but that was now totally out of the question, feeling the way I did. I was not sure which of the voices had spoken, when I heard, "You know, you should write."

With that, I quickly scribbled, "I, Lauviah, will remember everything I need to in the right space and time," and I signed and dated it. As I attempted to climb into bed, I could hear myself saying, "I want darkness." The light had become an invasion, and like a toddler screaming out in the supermarket in his quest for self-gratification, I wanted darkness, much the same without the strength, even screaming.

I was convinced that something big was happening to me because I could feel it in my bones, but I did not know what. I shut the blinds, but the sunlight was still intruding, so I grabbed a blue towel, which happened to be the exact size of the window, and stuck it with five white drawing pins ("Five: number of grace, and white: for purity"), with a star upon each head. As though I had been programmed to acknowledge the sequence of actions I had performed, which caused me to conclude that I was definitely in flow of what was developing.

I reached for a freshly washed cotton sheet, hoping to capture the usual welcome against skin, but as I slid under the cover, I felt as though I had climbed up the island's Morne Dugard instead of the bed. "I want more darkness!" So I covered my head and continued to breathe in deeply and exhale fully. "Lord, help me! Lord, help me!" I cried.

I don't recall ever having done so much asking as I did then.

"It was time to be granted my wish," I said.

Chatterbox, in a gently seductive voice, asked, "But didn't they say it is better to just be grateful than to ask?"

On hearing this, I thought, Is this not the same as when Satan said to Christ, "If you are the Son of God, why don't you turn these stones into bread?" Now, whether the timing of that thought made sense or not, that's what I felt.

Why was I hurting so much? I wondered what was causing my body to hurt so much? My chest and back felt like I had hit a six-inch-thick concrete wall, like the one in GPS.

Eventually, I was able to ease my back from the crunch and tension. The core deep inside had been most troubled and had left me to face with my own Final Destination Resort. So I delved in at an even deeper level with Resignation.

Between the tears that streamed down my face and the shower, I am not sure which had produced more wetness to my pillow. I always thought that the Psalmist King David was really exaggerating his pleas and groans to the Lord, thus making them seem well over the top, but now I think not.

The talks of the previous night with family and friends seemed to accompany each subsequent thought. People were reminiscing about their childhood experiences. The subject immediately got me thinking about losing my favourite person, Catherine, who happened to be the daughter of my mother's friend. I was not sure where I had been, but I can still see the outside of the day as I rushed into the house, like it was my home.

"What happen?" I asked.

"Catherine died."

"What that mean?"

"She just die."

No one would take the time to explain death to a child. I just knew I was very sad, and I missed my friend. That's too morbid, I thought. I can't talk about that. I don't recall agreeing to share my experiences, but it felt like a consensus had taken place and that I should do exactly like everyone else. I thought of how I had invited my lost friend into one of my counselling sessions and concluded that it was high time I let her remain in peace forever.

I wished for a pleasant early memory that would feel good to share. I was amazed that most people claimed to remember being as young as two. I knew it was not a competition, but I felt I had to say something. There was this other memory that never seemed to go away, but I wouldn't share even that. The circle around the table had heard everyone's account but mine. At that stage, I was angry that I did not have something to say. I did not want it to seem that I was avoiding the subject. I was also angry that I felt that I should have something to say. In addition, I could feel the food that I had enjoyed just moments ago was about to come up my throat.

I had recalled being lifted up into the high chair that I would sit in; each leg went through a separate space on either side. Maybe the bar across could be unclamped, but they did not bother to use it.

"What about you, Lauviah?"

With all eyes waiting, I laughed and said, "I am really amazed that you guys can actually remember as far back as being two and three; I must have been too traumatised to remember much." Why did I have to say that last part? I thought. Why did I have to say anything at all? And why do I keep wanting to remember anything more? I wrestled the thoughts out of my mind.

I removed the soaked sheet, still not fully unfolded, and turned the pillow over whilst pulling the cover higher over my head, to intensify the darkness. My God! Even that is a lot of work, I thought. I found myself turning from side to side, trying to find ease. What is the matter with me? I thought. I am now crouching like a baby in the womb. I think this is what they call cold turkey, like someone getting off heroin (I'd only seen it on television).

Chatterbox added, "Perhaps you are going through some kind of depression."

I was thinking of all sorts of things. Resignation, still very alert, reminded me that I would be alright, as long as I continued to trust the process.

So I said, "Spirit guide me, spirit lead me." Still, I wished for a gentle hand over my back; words need not be spoken.

No, I won't be calling anyone, I thought. Although I knew Zachiah would be delighted to oblige me, since he loves to immerse whomsoever he finds receptive, if given a jar of cream. But that would mean risk talking to someone, listening to someone, changing my position in the bed. No, no, I'll be fine, I told myself.

The question still remained as though I had made a covert agreement to not let go of the need to know what had caused my hurt. Surely it's not just those secrets. I hoped there were no more still hunting me. I wondered what it was.

What did I remember from my childhood? I cried a lot, but I also laughed a lot, too. Chatterbox and Resignation seemed to let me be. The two scenarios of Catherine and the blue high chair played hop-scotch in my mind; I had been left in there crying, with my arms stretched out, and no one would pick me up. I could see this picture of myself from an overhead view of the chair I had been sitting in. Perhaps that was the reason I never really liked the colour blue, but I was thankful to appreciate that it kept the light away. Catherine would have never let me cry so much without picking me up. Although I have no other memory of her, I felt she was always good to me.

"Wait a minute." I was trying to slow down the stream of information from Chatterbox and Resignation whilst another picture that I had deliberately put on the back-burner surfaced in my mind.

Mother had told me that she had left me with a baby-sitter and had gone to work, but on arriving home, the baby-sitter was gone, and she had no idea how long I had been left on my own. Mother said we were both lucky because I could have been burnt by the coal fire that was left on. Then, I could have been taken away from her.

I began to feel my body drifting and was trying not to think anymore. No more questions, I told myself, for everything I needed to know would come to me at the right time, right place, and right sequence. Then I said, "Lauviah, I am now allowing you to relax with Resignation," and I gently drifted. I had no idea how long I had drifted, or where exactly, but it was not sleep.

"No! No! No! No! No! No! No!" I could hear myself uttering an endless string of Nos, whilst agonising inside.

I could not tell for sure if it was Chatterbox or Resignation, but it was followed by "Yes! Yes! Yes! Yes! Yes! Remember, this is what you ought to be saying because it's the truth."

And at that moment, I remembered reading somewhere that when you encounter what you think is a disappointment or abuse of some kind, say yes to the universe and be thankful for the information. I think that's a brave thing to even write down, especially in this context. I could not contain the tears or the sound of my bawling; well, I tried. I had hoped that the noise of the TV would be enough to drown the sounds, but they came through from underneath the covers, and the other people could not hear me. I had been given a glimpse of what happened.

I continued bawling but still tried not be heard. "No, because it hurt, it hurt! He touched me! And it hurt! And all this time, I thought I was the lucky one to have escaped at a tender age." I felt compelled to utter the words as though my ears needed to hear them to believe, even though my heart still bled the scars.

No, I don't want them to see me cry. I don't want them asking why, I told myself.

So Mum knew all along?

It's really a crime when you don't have a voice, I thought. A real crime. In hindsight, it was so simple to work out; after all, I was not his child, and the fact that he did not spare his own ... how comes it took me so long to see and to work it out? He was the reason why I was sent to live with so many different people. Yes, I knew of incidences of when I was older, but at one? The revelation was definitely requiring stages of intervals to take in.

"I, Lauviah, give the universe total and complete permission to help me sleep. I just want to sleep, just sleep. I want to sleep," I lamented countless times. No expressions of gratitude, as previously suggested; none.

My soul cried out like I had not cried in a very long time. "Perhaps I can cushion my back with a pillow. I will pretend that someone is cuddling me and that someone is helping me to soothe my pain, even just a little," I said, trying to reassure myself.

Then, as though my eyes had turned inward, I could see different shades of blue, jagged shapes, round shapes, and scallop patterns, and some with no comprehensible order. The voice, which I think was Resignation's, whispered, "Just observe," and I knew the Crimson Light was in operation. Hence the phrase, "There is always light at the end of the tunnel."

"Yes, those blue lights again." I acknowledged their return, surrounded by illuminated crimson squares.

Its strangeness seemed to deliberately reassure me of its presence; a figure appeared as though it had walked through the window.

"Yes, I see you are okay," he said.

Where did he come from now? I wondered.

"Maybe you should get up now," Chatterbox said, in his faint tone.

I should have remained still and just observed. But instead, I opened my eyes, although I knew he'd be gone. Out of bed, and the clock said twelve fifty.

"I haven't eaten a thing; should I have breakfast now? At least try to eat something."

Was I looking for a reason to deny what I had seen? Yet, in my heart, I knew something, something grand or symbolic, was about to take place, and I certainly had no appetite for food. However, I wanted more darkness till I got back into bed with Resignation, with total submission, under the covers, whilst I prayed to be led by the Crimson Light.

Although feeling better than before, I still continued to breathe in deeply and exhaled fully.

I immediately shut my eyes and then made a conscious effort to utter my request: "Dear God, help me to sleep, just sleep, just sleep."

The colours returned in no time. With each attempt to sleep, Chatterbox and Resignation directed my attention by a gentle nudge: "Just observe."

Trying to make sense of it all, I saw breaks had appeared in the circles. I think it's about those energy patterns on the guided meditation I'd been following; I don't know for sure, but I heard "Breathe in deeply, now exhale fully."

Eventually, it felt like it had been just breath inside me. The air was now circulating through my lungs and ribs in a very blissful way.

"Lightness is here," I whispered. "The Crimson Light has got me feeling light, just light."

Now, I was just checking this sweet feeling in my heart, synchronising with my breath. My questioning seemed to have created a shift, so I continued to breathe in deeply and then exhaled fully.

"I am enjoying, perhaps I should say observing, that something is happening. My body is getting lighter and lighter. I have no sense of my limbs or of my body, but my heart and my head have become one," I observed.

I reminded myself to stay present because present is always a gift. I smiled to myself. This is good, I was thinking. But how is it that there is so much light, even while my eyes are shut under the cover? I remembered my teachers: "Just observe! Make no judgements," they said.

An indescribable pattern showed up, and I wanted to look at it. Immediately, I felt tingles on my face, as though demanding that I position my face upright, thus taking me out of the foetal position and onto my back. The tingles were more intense than I had experienced in any meditation. I had become accustomed to trusting the process; well, at least, that was my conclusion. Just as quickly, it was as though the grand master legends of the universe were moving my face. I could feel every nerve was being shifted, including the nerves and tissues around my eyes. I felt as though they were using a thousand volts, drilling and piercing straight through my forehead and onto the back of my neck, which in turn vibrated the whole of my scalp. I was definitely under arrest by this powerful force. I was totally surrendering with an audible "Zeeeeep. Zeeeeep." At that point, both Resignation and Chatterbox had been overpowered, too.

I could see the force coming from two lines that formed an angle: one from the heavens and the other from the horizon, but protruding straight from my head, forming an L-shape. Every neuron, every atom of my being had been touched. I could see the grids in the tunnel as though beckoning me closer, and I had become very alert.

I got up feeling light and looked into the mirror, like Zachiah would say, "What happen?" But there was no one to ask, "Did you see what happened?" Trying to make sense of my experience, I noticed my eyes had become really bright with increased vision. My skin was puffed as though I had the best Botox job done in the middle of my forehead. If only I could sell this stuff, I thought, but who'd be willing to pay the price? Then I wondered, Why do we always try to put a value of money on a thing? I suppose perhaps because there is a price to be paid for everything, and for many, money was our first conscious commodity. I also understood that one must be willing to pay the full cost for such an experience. No discounts or 50 percent off the marked price. It does not work like that. Whatsoever we sow, that shall we reap. It may seem fair to mention, due to the pain involved, that much or all of what happens in the process of sowing and reaping may prohibit one from submitting completely to the force. The important thing to remember is that the Crimson Light always remains committed to rewarding you accordingly.

Just savouring the experience of my eternal youth, I laid on the bed once more; then I was immediately zapped a second time by the force, with no restraint. I just totally resigned. Was I being abducted? It didn't matter; I had neither strength nor zeal to argue than to acknowledge the light, as I found courage in the mantra "Spirit leads me, spirit guides me."

I later found myself in a little gift-shop, topless, and there was one male and one female assistant behind the counter. With a slight degree of embarrassment, I covered my nipples with my palms while being served. To my amazement, and seeming out of nowhere, a towel was gently dropped onto my bare shoulders, wide enough to cover my upper body. In that precise moment, I knew that it was the Crimson Light assuring me that as a vital witness of Mr Barack Altidore's descent, I would always be protected, even if I were publicly cross-examined.

Then a third episode of the Crimson Light came zooming onto my face, and this time, it was as though a real major road reconstruction was taking place. I had no say in the matter, with just Resignation and even Chatterbox and I observing this major operation. I still had fleets of adoption stories pushing at the surface of my mind.

With the faintest of voice, I could hear myself saying, "Whatever," and if that really was the case, that I was truly being adopted, my secrets that I had written would be discovered. Then I realised perhaps that would be a good thing, if they'd tell it like it is.

With what little concern I had left, and as confirmation, Resignation said, "It's okay."

Chatterbox asked inquisitively, "What is okay? Being adopted by aliens? Is that okay? Or do you mean I'll be alright and still be in that head of yours, once this is all over?" At that point, I had absolutely no concern for either Chatterbox or Resignation.

Where did they come from? I do not know, but I was presented with a one-year-old child by three tall figures, whose faces I could not see and did not seem to care to know, either. This child came directly towards me, and I instinctively knew that my job was to protect her and reassure her of my love for her. As I beckoned her to me, I saw the most beautiful yet solemn face looking at me.

I said, "Come here, and look at me."

As she drew closer, her eyes mirrored mine to perfection. Whilst the left eye appeared brighter than the right, I wondered about its condition, but I quickly got my priority straight. With no hesitation, I uttered these words:

"I want you to know that anytime you see a flame, like this one in my hand, let it be a reminder of my love for you, because I am holding a flame in my heart at this very moment, and that flame is you."

Well, the next thing I knew, vroooooooooop: The little girl had horizontally entered the middle of my chest, just like that. It was just like when Mr Barack Altidore had been syphoned into the smoky hole, but at a much speedier rate.

There I was, the lovely child in my bosom, underneath my own skin, and her head to my left breast and legs over to my right breast, waiting to be cradled by me.

There was an inkling of wanting to reject this internal connection of being one with myself, but just as quickly as the thought had come, was an even quicker gesture of acceptance. I was pleased that I accepted me, because apart from the Botox job, yes, and the sense of lightness, I was glad I did not have to repeat the zaps and vrooooooooop module of the watch hour.

The Crimson Light is always offering us a choice. With both hands, I gently pressed her down into my bosom; I knew she was safe there. And I offered my words of praise: Let the child within me be joyous and say, "This is the day the Crimson Light has granted. I will rejoice and be happy in it!" I had cried unto the Lord, and he heard me out of his holy place and filled my heart with gladness.

Out of bed, I had really undergone some major soul work. Was it accidental? Or coincidental? Or synchrodestiny? That, I had safely traversed through the sublanes of the watchful hour of the eleventh day, of the eleventh month of my ritual. I was a bit dazed and weak, but I had no physical pain whatsoever.

For over fifty years, I had absolutely no idea what this little girl looked like, until then. And I had spent more than forty years in the wilderness, but admittedly, my awareness of that fact had been amiss. I just knew I was sad because of the absence of my connection with her.

The first ever photograph I knew of her was when she was sixteen years of age. I declare that I have now come to the end of my lamenting, thinking no one really cared to have taken a photograph of her as a child. All she had to go by was the mixed opinion that she was beautiful with curly hair and that she cried a lot and also laughed just as much, whilst some only remembered that she just loved to dance. She might have been all the above.

Now I have the real deal, a sense of self-identity. I can now obtain my boarding pass, for the Bridge of Actualising Self-full Love.

Anchoring Points

There are no accidents and no coincidences, but the choices we make:
Today, I am making a choice to see
myself,
others, and
realms.

I am now open and receptive to the guidance of the Crimson Light;
therefore, I am trusting the choice I have made to acknowledge
affects,
answers, and
aches.

My Holiness Is My Salvation

Since my holiness saves me from all guilt, recognizing my holiness is recognizing my salvation. It is also recognizing the salvation of the world. Once I have accepted my holiness, nothing can make me afraid. And because I am unafraid, everyone must share in my understanding, which is the gift of God to me and to the world.

—Helen Schucman, A Course in Miracles

CHAPTER 5

Bridge Construction

"There are no accidents and no coincidences, and remember this: Nothing happens by chance, but by choice! Nothing." I had made the choice to go into the school with the woman in black and observed the white-faced clock on the wall had showed eleven o'clock sharp, just before going off to sleep for an hour on the red couch. I also noticed that I had awoken at midnight to the bright Crimson Light all around. I was not afraid to step outside, for I had become one with the door that had beckoned me on. That's when I discovered that it was still very bright outside, and I saw the dogs, whose language I understood just like the six-inch-thickdoor.

I could breathe. Resignation gave me a nudge, his usual cue for my attention, by which I understood that not a lot happens without Resignation. An eclipse had taken place. Chatterbox's presence seemed completely overshadowed by Resignation's liveliness and extreme joy, like a warm sensation moving down my spine.

It was the revelation of the first hour of a new day and a new era. Instead of observing buildings and the cornfield in my head and Mr Barack Altidore stepping into the tombed casket, just like that, there was a sweet and gentle voice in my head: "I will give you the keys to the kingdom of heaven and onto the Bridge of Actualising Self-full Love, and whatsoever you shall bind on the earth shall be bound in heaven, and whatsoever you shall loose on the earth shall be loosed in heaven."

On hearing these words, all my attention turned inward, with little regard to my surroundings.

The absence of Chatterbox fostered the gravity of my engagement with Mr Altidore, and I began to imagine, What if his descent were an actual ascension? And what would it look like?

Suddenly, a six-foot veil with pink and silver shades of light appeared directly in front of me. And like the warm greeting of the dogs, I felt safe. Followed was my total amazement at Resignation's tone, which sounded more like an excited child opening a Christmas gift.

"Lauviah, this is Presence, one of the elders."

She gently unveiled her head, revealing a wide smile that immediately filled my heart with delight. And in her deep yet eloquent voice, Presence said, "Hello, my dear child, welcome on board, and so glad you are here."

My attention was captured by the ceremonial entrance of six other veiled figures, who had taken their positions, three on either sides of Presence. I got the feeling they were expecting me, just like the two dogs outside GPS, but with one difference: The elders did not walk away; instead, they surrounded me as though I were on display.

Without shifting her gaze, Presence continued, "You might have figured by now, we are the seven pillars that construct the bridge of this sphere." The verbal introduction continued with Presence, as each elder took their turn and bowed in reverence as Faith, Truth, Unity, Conviction, Forgiveness, and Endurance. I was captivated by their warmest inexplicable embrace, one in essence that touched every cell in my body and every breath that I took. Now, just like Sleeping Beauty, in her waking to a kiss, so was my awakening, definitely not to be missed.

Are they here for me like we had been for Mr Barack Altidore? I thought. And if so, what is it that I am I meant to do?' Since I no longer have any inclination to step into a tomb. On the contrary, I felt quite elevated in my spirit.

Though in awe, a part of me yearned for a confirmation that I had not gone insane. If it were so, that would mean my operation in GPS, and my witness to Mr Altidore's descent, including my confession, would all be unreal. Please tell me I have not gone insane, I thought. I became aware that like Chatterbox, Resignation had disappeared. I was on my own with the elders.

I had met Presence many times before, but I was unaware of the fullness of her radiance, which became more apparent in her dialogue as though responding to my prayer:

"Why am I here?"

"The answer, my sweet child, always lies in the position of your question.
As flip sides of the coin, or even if you were to ask of me, 'Why are you here?'
My first response would be, to let you know that my position is real. Presence.

"I am the force responsible for the vision of your inspiration to be here.
When you close your eyes and you see a flash of your life's dreams and desires,
You ask, 'Why?' But the answers you find also explain how.
And you wonder ... Yes, it is I.
You must know this: I am the flowers that you gaze on each passing day,
And even the ones that you touch as though not real,
For further confirmation you bend down, and you not only squeeze

But quickly take a sniff.

"'Inexplicable,' you say, as I poise with a display of my arrays of
beauty.
Look at your clothes, curtains, and varying contours.
I am the bright coloured robes that you wear,
Though your friends, they won't dare.
I am your unshakable Presence, even in the midst of your storm;
Full of potentiality, for all creativity must exert through your
emotions,
Right here in me, but then, I become your concept.

"I am the transparent seas that you behold in the eyes of the
child,
Of the mother and the father, the brother and the sister;
The friend and, if you will agree, even the foe.
Through all these you will know, this is how you grow.
The joys you perceive in all transparent seas,
If you ever care to know: with each enlargement of your heart,
And the standing of hairs upon your back,
And with shivers flooding down your spine,
Like the feel of morning dew under your bare feet,
As you wonder why and how,
You are in awe, to have found the answer,
Ah yes! It is I.

"Yes, you will find me amongst the trees;
And in the forest and the sounds of the gusty winds.
I am also the gushing waters flowing down streams,
And as you prostrate to your knees and utter, 'Yes please,'
You hear the words right from the depths of your soul,
Though not aloud: 'Yes, you are healed.'

"I am the mystic in the air, between the rainbow and this sphere.
I am the taste to your palate, for a reminder that the food you
partake
Is not only of your sweat, but indeed, also of the other.
I am the tune that you hear soothing your head,

Whilst protecting you from despair.

"I am present in the dark of the night
And even when you take an aeroplane flight.
It is vital that you know 'as above, so below,'
For darkness shall become light and light shall be dark,
And the two shall be one;
For the lips of the East and the lips of the West
Must come together to perform my optimum best.

"I am the twirling of the autumn leaf, though cold, you stop and
stare;
And you gain the insight of the seasons
And discover that everything is really for a reason.
I am the joys in your beating heart, and with each cackling of a
laugh,
Though often used for the covering of a wound,
And yet even then, I am amazed of the intensity of your pain;
But somehow, you still find your gain.

"I am your index finger in the palm of the newborn babe;
Though you have been there countless times,
Still you are in awe, as you say, 'I can't believe that was me.'

"I am the miracle winemaker of many moons ago, enabling your
feast;
Even though often goes unnoticed through your cash payments
of various currencies.
I can be presently majestic, super-duper and fantastic,
Though at times you may find me somewhat lethargic.
But I can assure you, I am always here.

"I am the birds that greet you and motivate you with a morning
song
As you look out your window pane and you behold the morning's
rain.
And yes! I am the shelter above your head.
Yet, I am the warmth when you raise your face to the sunrise

That welcomes you to another day's surprise.
But just remember, when I am set, it doesn't mean I'm gone,
Because I am also the moon, whether or not you still see me at
noon.

"Digression or progression, either of these you choose; I am still
in your face.
Let me tell you, my dear child, it is always best to wear a smile.
For drowning excuses will only provide a disappointing place to
hide.
Though often I show up in what you call death,
And yet solemn inside, I still manage to cause you to reciprocate
a smile.
That is why you can also find me in marketplaces
Bantering prices as though they were sky high,
But this is only to ignite my warm spark inside.
And still, many hide,
While others shout, 'Hey! Your price is much too high.'

"I can be warm and yet I can be cold.
That depends on the perspective and the attention you give me.
Hence, my wish for you is to always remember
I perform best when I am warm.
So it is important to know that the degree of intention
Is the determining factor of what equals the sum of your
experience in me."

Now, typical of Presence, with the warmest smile ever, she
ended her teaching with these words: "Remember, my dear
child of the Open University of Life, as long as you are here,
everything given to you must be received in my spirit as 'present,'
for this is where true Wisdom lies.

"For if you look well, you will be able to tell, that it is I,
Presence, sent as gifts to you.
Hence, cherish me well.
For every smile that you meet and every experience endured,
There I am in the midst of it all.

Therefore, it is only fair to say, even though sometimes only in spirit,
I am here because you have Presence. Ha! Ha! Ha!"

Now if I understand well, one thing for sure is that Presence is, in fact, everywhere.
It almost seemed a bit unfair to mention Chatterbox, the information collector whose charisma, when at best, had somewhat reminded me of Presence. But why isn't he here? I wondered.
With arms swaying whilst moving her hips and teasing with her eyes,
Presence penetrated my heart and caused me to smile as the words rang against my ears:
"And still I rise," which felt like a seed that had been planted in me,
That I would anticipate my own rise, my voice, I would no more hide.

"Pardon me, Presence, but might I say you did not mention romance?
Is it true that it is all in the dance?"

"My dear sweet child, did you not know that
embracing all your life's experiences is, in fact, the main form of romance?
And as you move from desperation to acceptance of my inspiration,
You'll surely learn how to dance, to the sounds of all life's drums.
The more you practice, the better you'll become at singing and swinging as you romance. (Singing and swinging? Wasn't that Maya Angelou? I thought).
Just ensure to be wise in all your steps and make me the grand choreographer of your dance."

I was in awe, and even if I tell you, perhaps you can't imagine the joy I felt by just being with Presence, who seemed to have always been near; only that I had been unaware.

As she said, "Remember, I am yours.
Presence."

Faith, veiled in bright orange, representing her will to prolong our lives, greeted me with the brightest of smiles. A lot like Presence's loving spark, Faith ignited a fiery blaze in her mouth, as she blurted out, "I am immeasurable."

For my lesson, Faith warned me to embrace the teaching of Jesus Christ, particularly in the parable of the mustard seed. She said, "Likewise, I am not just a mustard seed. I am a 'must-add' ingredient, as the gift to help bring about all your desired outcomes. However, you can find me in both great and small seeds, as even in seemingly insignificant kindness. Remember, they also ripple into effects of miraculous acts.

"So you can see, I not only deal with issues of sexuality and relationships, I also help people to free themselves of guilt and recognise their creativity."

Now, just as I was thinking, Is it only the teachings of Jesus Christ that Faith works with? she looked me straight in the eye and said, "Would I be so foolish to work for only you? My purposeful acts would be rather limited if I did not have all the other Faith schools to be of service to. After all, isn't that what makes me so dynamic?"

You may enjoy her smile, but Faith can wipe it off in a flash just like that, as she never fails to remind the world, "I am the substance of the seed that you have conceived in thoughtful dreams, as you go to sleep, or choose to seek, or perhaps hear from the pulpit. Come! Come over here. Here is your mustard seed, for I am the evidence of things you believe will come to pass and will no longer be a dream."

Faith has a way of demanding your attention just to ensure that you are following her instructions and directions as she explains, "I am telling you this for your own good. Did you know that I am also the seeds laid down in the ground? Sometimes even with just a little care, I rise up, and behold, the evidence is in various foods decoratively placed on your table."

Faith continued, "Now I need to say this: I know you've done your best, but why in heaven's name did you take so long to confess?"

And with a deep breath I said, "Wellll …" I was hesitant because I was not sure whether it was a rhetorical question or not. As far as I was concerned, most evidently, I had done the work to getting onto the Bridge of Actualising Self-full Love. I soon found out that I did well to not rush my response. It turned out, this was just Faith's humour talking like that.

"But seriously," she added, "I wish people realised how hard I actually work to make life better for them. If only they would trust me more. They often say they do, but they are not sure if they are worthy of me. This is just total nonsense. The few, on the other hand, who feel worthy of me are unaware that by trying to keep me a secret, they do a dis-service not only to others, but also to themselves. In essence, they don't trust anyone, and therefore, they cannot gain Truth or Conviction in order to have Endurance to accomplish their goals."

Since I had been there, what could I do but to just listen? Moreover, Faith is so interesting; you can never have too much of her. Once you've seen the evidence of her acts, you begin to appreciate Faith is just like dynamite.

"See, people have not understood the principles I operate under. It is a clear-cut rule," Faith continued. "Just do your utmost best by firstly ensuring the end of your desire in mind, and the Crimson Light will do the rest. Now, be mindful, there are those who know how I operate so well that they even know how to use me for unfavourable deals. You see, the trouble is, once they've done the work, what can I say? You have to do the work. However, the outcome in such cases only lasts until they come round full circle, by which they are forced to review the other side of the coin, because I am fair all around."

I was thinking apart from Faith and Presence working together, they must be closely related. They seemed to share the same characteristics, but with one difference: Faith is tactile and likes to hold on to you. One could say it's her way of making herself available, so that you know it's alright to hold onto her. On the other hand, you can feel Presence by just the mention of her name.

Faith is not boastful, but charismatic, and perhaps one might even add somewhat dramatic at times. Her trust in you is important; otherwise, you could easily go insane, thus losing the opportunity to hold or lean onto her for your world's gain. That is why we go through many tests until we discover all things are possible with Faith.

Faith reassuresd us that apart from Truth, Conviction, and Endurance as her closest allies, she does absolutely nothing without Unity. "Furthermore, I will let you in on a secret," Faith said. "Numerous people have succeeded in fulfilling their dreams and desires, but not one of them made it without me. Sometimes, you might hear someone say, 'I can't believe it.' Or 'I didn't really think I would ever make it.' In those cases, I extend myself through another elder, so as to make people more susceptible to me; I just dedicate myself in different ways."

When I heard this, I was moved.

The amazing thing about Faith is this: Sometimes, she does not even require a lot from us, but mainly to believe or to just make a declaration of our willingness to embrace her (or perhaps allow her to embrace us).

"Take, for instance, the well-known story of Norman Cousins, who it was believed was sick and dying. All the man did was shift his attention onto Faith and presumably paid his forgiveness bill. He watched funny movies all day, and he was healed. Now I ask you, is this a brand deal?"

When Faith told me that, oh God, I laughed.

People have actually held onto the hem of Faith's garment and gotten healed because Faith really yields. Take the example of Louise Hay; it was felt that she would transit into another realm soon after being diagnosed with cancer. Along with Faith, she not only healed her life but went on teaching the rest of the world through five words: "You Can Heal Your Life."

Now what I like most about Faith is, she's always willing to direct us to Forgiveness, so we, too, can learn how to behave compassionately towards others.

Some people, however, seem to get in the habit of falling flat on their faces in their attempt to be with Faith. So I asked her how she made sense of these perpetual face-flattening individuals.

"Huh! Face-flattening individuals!" Faith looked at me and smiled, as though recognising one standing right before her eyes. "I leave them theire until they are ready to get their acts together." She said she often raised their heads to her breast and cradled them in her arms, just to find a moment's rest, "and after that, my God, they know they must progress."

But some people like her breast so much, they just keep falling flat on their faces, just to keep going back. According to Faith, it is at those times she calls for Forgiveness and whispers, "Forgive them, for they know not what they do by expressing such lack in me."

Now, after such a demonstration, they often consult with Truth and Unity, and with Conviction, they find Endurance. This is what's often called a miracle.

Now I understand, it is by performing those acts of faith that the elders themselves attain a good rapport. On hearing this, I just remained steadfast, as she ended her teaching: "Remember, I am yours.

Faith."

Truth, with a sunlit veil uncovered, shines on everything and everyone. He said that his nature is all about realism and also reveals the illusions that we choose as real. His job, basically, is about knowingness and putting things into their right perspectives. Truth shows his nature and the attributes of humankind through countless historical accounts (even fables). He also takes on the form of the Holy Bible, the Koran, the Tao, the Bhagavad Gita, and more, teaching humankind how to know God. And that is, in essence, a demonstration of his audacious spirit. You can experience him as heavy or light. It all depends on your receptivity and exploration of Truth. To know Truth for yourself, according to him, whatever the situation, you must be willing to face him naked.

"I am the way and the Crimson Light,
No one comes to the place of resolution or absolution but by me.
I am, therefore, the elements of life: the air that you breathe,
The light that sustains, including the ground that you walk upon,
And not only the water that you drink but also the great parting of the seas

"That you've heard about so many moons ago.

I am that which flooded the earth
And has left its residue in the out-pouring of your heart.
Therefore, I am not only every drop in the ocean,
But even in your teardrop too.
I am simply energy of life,
So if you care to know, I am in all your operations,
For it is me who brings you peace.

"I am the fire of the Potter's house.
That is how you know you've been touched by me,
Although I am also the drought on the land,
Whose blight, I am still able to quench.

"It is I, Truth, knocking on your heart's door and crying out loud,
Let me out! Let me out!
How do you expect me to stay in here?
Look at the condition of this place.
Just take a look at me; I am clean.
I am neat and sharp as a blade,
And don't even bother to compare me with that Hollywood Blade.
We are not the same; he's simply child's game.
Therefore, it is not because you see me smile that it gives you the right
To try and take off my eyes so I would not have to see you hide.
Uh! That could never be!

"It is often said of me, what the eyes see, the heart won't feel;
Now, take careful note of what I say to you:
Don't be fooled by believing that you can just commit all kinds of sins,
Because you won't get away with it.
Often, I am used to become whatever you will.
Just remember, it is I, Truth, that lets you know
By showing the real nature of the heart,
That it's actually the place where all manner of ills reign.
However, it is also the place where all goodness can prevail.

"I beckon you, don't mess with me.
Because I can toss you so far.
You wouldn't know what hit your solar plexus,
As you bawl out, 'This is insane.'

"Take a look from outside. I can preserve you from the cold,
But I can also scald you so severely till you burn.
Sometimes my heart is just a reaction that you need to take better care of yourself
So that you don't end up feeling despair or what you call heartburn or a heart attack.
That is why I advocate that you love me with all your being,
Even as the father above and mother earth love me.
While I continue to light up in your life so that you, too,
can experience for yourself how much our father and mother love you.
More so, when you function daily with me inside,
You will come to know thyself and do thyself no harm.

"I am the burning bush often spoken of; my wish for you, through Moses,
That you can simply light a candle and find me while you stare.
When you wake up in the morning and you look to the horizon,
You gleam at the size and shades of my eye,
By which you behold my existence lies in everyone else's eyes.
As your gaze gets quickly shortened by the fierceness and rage of my heat,
You blink your eyes into retreat, and discover
I am truly light over everything.
Sunglasses? Ah, but I know whose eyes are behind them.
Because I have been formed in knowledge
Stands the reason why I dwell everywhere.

"I do admit that sometimes I behave slowly in revealing myself
But that is only to allow you to grow,
While others attempt to ridicule me, of course,
Hoping some people will see them bright.
Don't they know there is no bigger light than mine?
They have obviously gone blind.

"I am also that which dwells with Presence,
So you can also find me in witty inventions,
Just showingtwo ways of how to know God.
Otherwise, how would you pass the criteria to getting onto the
Bridge of Actualising Self-full Love? Since I am also that which
ignites the fire of the Crimson Light.

"I am the direction one should follow and abide by,
The implicit knowing and being with Conviction.
Therefore, it is my transparency that gives a weightless
Yet profound sense of actualising self-full love."

Truth continued in his declaration, "I know that many have used
me to departmentalise and label other individuals, groups, and
organisations against the very message I am here to convey.
Let me make it clear: I dwell in not just some, but in every one of you.
Therefore, whenever you have faced the Crimson Light, you have
faced me.

"Sometimes, I am taken with a pinch of salt,
But in all essence, I am simply like a sweet-smelling fragrance,
An undeniable scent; everyone must try to identify themselves in me,
As that which quickens your bodies reflects the beauty of the Crimson
Light.

"People wonder why so often they experience me through low to
high voltages.
It's the Crimson Light's way of preparing you in accordance
For the healing of the rupture that caused you pain.
Attempts are made to drown me in a bottle or hide me behind
weight issues
Or numbness through drugs or putting up smoke screens,
With a host of excuses to validate your action or inactions,
Thus pretending I'm really not there.

However, I warn you: Regression or suppression, I am still in your face,
As long as there remains a human race.

"Do you not see me? Do you not feel me? I am right here; look
within you.
I could have you rewired in no time, but how would you know that
I really exist?

"Even when you hear someone say 'I can smell a rat a mile away,'
I not only speak the language of five senses but others more profound.
You may even choose to share me in a stench,
For this is a certain way of knowing the state of your affairs.
Hence, I say, death or life, make amends, and cherish the smiles.
It may mean a dying of self, including the indulgences and pleasures,
As a slaying of the primal needs to render love perhaps to a child.
Hereafter, one might say love equals death from the other side."

It was then I saw that Mr Barack Altidore's descent was indeed an
expression of scented love in action. The Crimson Light is more
evident, with its irresistible, brilliant rays kindling our spiritual
synaptic nerves through Truth; in turn, it brings us back into a sense
of oneness. This often takes place, according to Truth, through a
smile, a touch, or a gaze into one's eyes that says "I care." Then Truth
connects us to strangers who are no more, showing us the way to
getting onto the Bridge of Actualising Self-full Love.

Truth ended his teaching: "Knowing my dwelling place is in the
heart, you can be assured that where I am, there you may be also.
Hence my purpose for teaching you how to know God.
Remember, I am yours.
Truth."
Gently draping the long blue veil off her face, Unity enthralled my
heart as she began her message. It was a perfect reminder of my quest:
to one day find a voice of such sounding clarity, trust, and sincerity,
thus reaching the soul.

"You can call me abundance," Unity said, "for this is what I do:
I represent all potentiality to increase. I a m not just one unit
but infinitely whole. You will find me in perfect harmony, where
separation was once the game, but is no more. No more fights, as
though you were insane, but now are on a different plane. That's why
you hear 'United we stand; divided we fall.'

"I am Unity in every form of life: in the grafting of the tree;
And in the embryo of the womb, creating stability for the life inside;
Causing two to not only seem one, but harmoniously live as one.
Hence, my work is a lot like Faith's and Presence's,
Constantly in agreement, establishing common ground for motion,
In succeeding our passion, and to attain the desired outcome of the
vision.

"I am the ink to your paper; the glue that was once licked onto the
back of your letter.
Although not used so frequently nowadays, nevertheless, I am your
foundation,
Like the movement of your tongue to your palate, whether around
food or speech.
You still don't miss the perfection of your intention.
And yet, I am the sepulchre accommodating the rest for your transit,
Even as the sounds to your ear, as you move your head to the harmony
that you hear,
Or a gentle tap on your shoulder; you respond to the words 'Hello,
my dear.'

"I am both the dressmaker and the fine robe you wear,
As you utter, 'This one was made just right for me.'"

Unity said that she is the energy that existed at the time of birth,
Including the palms of the hands, the smiles and utterances shared,
whenever one exclaimed, "It's a boy!" or "It's a girl!"

Unity exerts her position in the welcome of a kiss and the embrace of mother to child, and even the energy from the tiny fingers imposed and the coordination of the first steps and the first words spoken of the infant.

"I am the thread that holds every relationship,
Between siblings, husband and wives, including neighbours and friends and lovers, too."

Unity is the hermaphroditic energy that knows the weighing of our spirits
And helps us to balances them out. It is she who marries people, communities, countries, and continents, through games of peaceful activities. Unity says it is she who sits in agreement at round tables in issues of sports and political affairs. She sees through red tape and lends the right suitability in line of their compatibility, for one spirited plan: only to unite.

That is why with Unity, we become victorious, regardless the form, as long as there is agreement. Unity warns us to make our thoughts clear so that our hearts can be in alignment with our intentions. Be mindful in your dialogue and honour the tongue, as she often demonstrates it's the most powerful muscle you can possess. Treat it with sweet and tender loving words from the heart, and let it heal us. Likewise, if you dishonour that gift with harsh and abrasive words, or ill intentions, it can pierce hearts and even kill you. In essence, wherever you find the spirit of agreement, Unity says, "I am there also."

People have low-based needs, often referred to as "negativity." However, this is only meant for the purpose of meeting our primitive needs by which one is able to make distinctions for high-based needs, often referred as positive. Truth reflects through our lives. Like Resignation, Unity requires our full consent to operate. But be mindful of half-consents, for they tend to qualify a request that conflicting outcomes derive from contrasting energy base levels. Ultimately, this in turn becomes like a plug connected to the wrong circuit box or an appliance with an inappropriate voltage capacity. Therefore, bear in mind that Unity's purpose at all times is to unite.

Unity ended her teaching by reminding us of the words so often spoken: "We are more alike than different."

Remember, I am yours.

Unity."

Conviction is the predominant masculine energy, whose passion is to succeed at whatever Truth sets in his heart. It is he that is conceived by our affirmed ideas, followed by immediate actions in acknowledgement of all divine purposes. It is he who says, "Thy will be done." Disciplined by dedicated minds and trained in all kinds of combat, Conviction has earned an array of badges and medals of honour in his name. He is the everlasting gift expressed in Presence and executes judgements for that which must be. His determined spirit is the driving force evident in the deliverance of your every desire. Conviction is the chauffeur always willing to use whatever resources necessary for achieving our quest. To his every victory, regardless how small, each step draws one nearer to the Bridge of Actualising Self-full Love.

Conviction is the gut feeling that makes you want to say, "Yes, I do." And with his regimental allies such as Endurance, Truth and Faith alongside, you will also hear him say, "Even if it kills me ..." because deep down, he knows that there is no dying of the soul.

Although audacious in his approach, Conviction can also be discreet in preparation for that which he must meet. He commands balance and respect for his attention to ensure that we yield in his direction. He often warns us that it is important we acknowledge him in every journey with Endurance because of the dis-ease that we often experience in the process.

Conviction says that he operates like a foetus inside the womb; you cannot ignore nor suppress him because the morning sickness and contractions are certain to let you know he is there. He gives further warning for what he says must be the preparation for his confinment and delivery: to ensure the clearing of our energy points, even with simple practice of meditation. He stressed that this clearance is important because he hates the idea of being mistaken for a gastric gripe, seeking to ease. He gives us the ability to rise through sheer determination to maintain our course.

Bearing in mind that Conviction has the ability to deal with both sides of the coin, we are called not to judge, for such interference may only disturb the flow of miracles to be performed. And according to Conviction, this practice is indeed the peace that passes all understanding.

As I listened, I felt as though Conviction sounded quite radical in his approach, but wasn't it Clint Eastwood as Dirty Harry who once said, "A man's got to do what a man's got to do"? I suppose that's Conviction for you.

Standing his ground, balanced and strong, and without further explanation, Conviction blurted into the song: "I am what I am and what I am needs no explaining." At the end of his tune, Conviction took a bow and exclaimed, "You don't have to do anyone else, just do you.

"Remember, I am yours.

Conviction."

Forgiveness looked at me with eyes that seemed to reach way down my soul as she explained, "It is through me that you learn how to give graciously, and I in turn provide the opportunity to receive joyously, as a way of loving your body, mind, and spirit. It is where you often say 'killing two birds with one stone,' but instead, I say to you, it is far better to consider 'saving two souls with one word:

Forgive.' There in my name lies the power to break down the walls of pride, especially when you realise you just can't hide. I am undeniably the prerequisite to attaining peace and joy."

Forgiveness is the spiritual undertaker, for she does not give a hoot about what state that she finds you in, just as long as you are with Resignation.

Are you in shame and feeling blamed for the repercussions of that guy Fear? Remember, shame and blame are games often played by overenthusiastic teachers and students of the Open University of Life, eager to prove their competence to teach and learn, rushing the modules of "Self Actualisation" In turn, they exert unnecessary force in the process, hoping they do not have to repeat them, but ending up causing pain to their nearest and dearest in the long run.

To ensure they succeed, they roleplay multiple times, ensuring to improvise just so that it could be said that theirs was "to take the mic." That's when others have decided to make a joke at your expense, not taking into account you might be new at the game.

While it seemed like weakness, you become strong because you know that you're not wrong.

I said, "Yes, I know just what you mean. It's just like one day Yvonne was banging my head against the wall for no apparent reason; in that very moment, I called on your name: 'Oh, please forgive her! For I think she might have gone insane,' and in that very moment, you gave me peace, and I felt quite strong."

Forgiveness said, "People find me hard to accept, but really, I do not bite. What is often experienced as a blow to the solar plexus is really Pride trying to hide what is truly inside. For example, there was a young man and his mother on The Oprah Winfrey Show, a very sad interview, I thought. He was the brother of the late singer Whitney Houston, who felt responsible for his sister's death because he introduced her to drugs. He was asked whether he thought that he might ever be able to free himself of the burden of his guilt. It seemed to me that my brother in question may have heard of my power, but he just dismissed me at will. I wish he really knew me and explored his chance for freedom; instead, his answer was a frantic, 'No, never.'"

On hearing this, I felt sadness for the man in question because I know what happiness one stands to gain by taking a chance on Forgiveness.

"Acceptance of self, family and background, community, and country of the world is crucial, to permit the opportunity to honour yourselves and others, so that your days may be sweet in the land of the living. Even when logic fails and you proceed to sabotage the sweetness of peace, I will endeavour to grant you ease, by directing you to Faith and Truth. Either route you may take to this triad is always the offer to lighten your soul in the perfect splendour of Crimson Light."

Therefore, it's never a joke to hear Forgiveness is the key to the opening of any heart.

Day or night, you can heal your life.

Remember, I am yours.
Forgiveness."

As Endurance drew closer to me, it felt like my heart had become so filled with serotonin that it was now overflowing. Although there seemed to be an air of supremacy about him that commanded the attention, even of God, yet his was the humblest of souls I had ever met. The purple veil across his shoulder gave the impression that it had been spindled by an angel.

His voice was distinct as I heard him say, "I see you made it onto the Bridge of Actualising Self-full Love," at which point, I simply melted by the rays of his smile. It was as if he had found something like himself in me on which he was attached to.

Since nothing happens by chance but by choice, then you must know there is no victory gained without Endurance at the end.

"People often make the mistake of giving up too soon because of what they perceive is the absence of my appearance. They don't realise that their development with each elder is indeed crucial for the service to them. Of course, depending on degree of need, I show up in phases. In which case, one could say I am multifaceted, since I exist like six separate selves." Uh? Thank God I'm not the only one actually experiencing this 'separate selves' business now."

This was someone I can really relate to, I thought, and continued to listen: "I like to know I can keep my word and maintain my will to be strong. However, this does not mean I am about throwing my weight around, because everything and everyone is important to me. Hence the reason, whilst it may be seen as though I only work on the logical side that most think is right, I work on both sides of the coin.

"My role is to engage with all parties and with one objective in mind, which is to bring peace and light to the whole world through humankind. I know what it's like to not have peace. Take for instance the host who dedicated money and their voices for world peace. That, I must say, gave me the sweetest feeling inside."

Endurance spoke of countless unhealthy battles in wars that produced disharmony of separateness of minds of persons, groups, and countries. According to Endurance, "It is important to overcome our individual wars so that we will progress."

I thought, That make sense because it must have felt like a gunshot blasting in Euyah's face when I left him standing at the registry's office that day. Anyway, now that I have overcome many battles through the Crimson Light, I want to leave all that right where it belongs, flowing under the Bridge of Actualising Self-full Love.

I was so relaxed with Endurance as he told me, "I am glad to see that our work together has finally paid off."

I felt so good that my heart instantly inflated with love for him; even then, I needed to be with Endurance, for my sustained joy was almost overbearing.

"Perhaps some would rather skip your journey, but look: You are here! I know there were times you thought I had ceased to exist, but now you know why I seemed distant when you were low. It's because I knew you had Faith to carry on. I also knew you had tested my longevity and staying power, time and time again. As you have now proven for yourself they may pronounce me dead, but I'll always be here, even as each day's sunrise."

Endurance spoke of his story of suffering and pain, whilst accompanying us through the many repercussions of life's choices we make, whether conscious or unconscious.

Then it dawned on me, that my witness to Mr Barack Altidore stepping into the tombed casket, just like that, had been the answer to my prayer. I had prayed to know him. I had prayed to know Endurance. "Oh my God, I am in awe of your faithfulness towards me," I said.

In that instance, the sounds of my own words revealed, not only that Mr Altidore was with Truth and Conviction who served as witnesses, stepping into the tombed casket, just like that, but his act could only have been performed as that of Endurance. Now, this wasn't just mind movies playing, but my soul was moved by what I saw before me: It was the movie, The Prophecy of Endurance.

Yes, I saw that his life had demonstrated true character, and he possessed a range of skills and talents, such as kindness, humility, meekness, and long-sufferingness. For this reason, although he was deemed a criminal by lesser minds, he performed many miracles with Conviction.

The movie depicted the human spirit, when crushed by painful emotions, is like the process of crushing grapes to make wine: thus, he was trampled upon. Once a person is healed, she experiences life's blissfulness and can hardly escape the essence of an "Ah" exclamation, as though having tasted the best of wines. Often, this happens without the slightest inclination of regret for the pain that has been endured. Thus, a legacy is birthed through curious minds that wonder just how he survived. But because Faith is always with Endurance, the reason why is that he is seen as a big brother who many simply continue to trust.

On observing any battle, one might say, "Let's see who is going to win." It is important to note that with Endurance, everyone wins in the end, just to show that we are all of the same vine. He also encourages us to observe how Unity and Truth coexist in a group, such as families, towns, countries, and so on. Although many leave home and return as mature individuals, remember you are de-vine, in essence, even better than good wine.

Still, with Conviction, Endurance beckons us to increase our awareness of all goodness in the earth. He prophesied if we follow this rule, we would in turn perform even mightier acts than he had done because every vine must bear each season after its kind.

Endurance used great words of wisdom that not only rattled but penetrated even the toughest of hearts. Whilst some people were fascinated by the depth of his knowledge, others simply called him mad. It was he who also spoke of Forgiveness, instead of the attitude of "an eye for an eye, and a tooth for a tooth." How else could we live amongst ourselves without Endurance, to see with our eyes and to share our smiles with each other?

One must have Endurance through Conviction and a willingness to die of the self. This, however, ought to be with the intention that the journey for each generation will become easier for the Bridge of Actualising Self-full Love. Now since I had found myself there, it must have proven that I was certainly willing to die. Perhaps I really did, since I found myself in a totally different realm.

The second half of the movie: The Prophecyof Endurance had borne the same hallmark as, a bridge to Actualising Self-full Love and had shown parallels of the part I had to act. For instance, we were each not fathered by husbands of our immediate homes. That left both mothers to wonder, "What will people say, since I am now with child, conceived by another?" The complicated circumstances meant we had to move away from the geographical place of inception, before making our entrance into the world. Some people had pronounced terrible things against Endurance: that he would give up his glowing cloak of the Crimson Light and worship a lesser god. Likewise, Mr All-Bags-Full and many others had prophesied that my life would be a blight, like Jezebel.

He was the coffin-maker's son. Whilst I, on the other hand, was the daughter of dress-maker who provided life's essentials for the journey we must make till one is laid in the tomb.

He had a friend named Lazarus whom he had raised from the dead after four days; I dealt with another.

Lazarus the grave-digger, whom I discovered in a roundabout way, was also my friend, but it was he who helped to raise me from the dead.

Endurance had spent forty days and forty nights in the desert. For the duration of that time, along with Faith, but through the abstinence of sexual pleasure, anyone can see that was sufficient to be termed a desert in itself, and still, I prayed.

He felt rejected by his own family but regarded the disciples as his own. I felt the same, having lived from one home to the next in a quest to feel I belonged. There were times the locals were not interested in his message: to share love. A dream I also held dear, for the people of St Lucia and the whole world to know they, too, can Actualise Self-full Love.

Endurance was perhaps as much in the valley as the mountaintop. This, in turn, not only made him a companion but also a good champion, guiding us even when we are on the edge, since he knew what it felt like to be there. Hence, we are reminded that through our adversities, we get the insight of the essence of patience to achieve true greatness. Such has been the graph of my life, being in constant motion, as I travel up and down life's course that shows me "Yes, I can," even on this plane, to declare the evidence of my existence.

He was seen as crazy because he would not hide the magnificence of who he was and insisted on doing what he was meant to do. Endurance's magic, by far, exceeds the acts of putting body parts back together, as often displayed on your television screen, but rather, his specialty is to connect souls as one. Just like him, I will not hide from being the person I am meant to be and do what I am here to do, even though I had been tested under a variety of life's conditions.

Now it's often said that Endurance is the main trainer of the Open University of Life, through which we are able to conjure up the courage to overcome all trials and tribulations.

It is therefore easy to see how, throughout generations, he continues to have large gatherings of followers calling out his name. He holds the torch that helps ignite our spark inside as he reminds us that we are the light of the world. In addition, Endurance beckons us to appreciate the power within: the beliefs that propel us to achieve our goals. This, in turn, indicates the importance of cultivating and changing our beliefs as necessary to succeed.

And with these closing words, Endurance said, "I have come that you will be the best that you can be and to live abundantly.

"Remember, I am with you always.
Endurance."

Aha! I had been in the company of the elders, the universal grand masters who exist in our race. Their various skills not only helped me actualise self-full love but unlocked the magnificence of the bridge construction.

Anchoring Points

There are no accidents and no coincidences, but the choices we make:
Today, I am making a choice to see
love provide,
love attract, and
love nourish.

I am now open and receptive to the guidance of the Crimson Light;
therefore, I am trusting the choice I have made to
acknowledge love,
appreciate love, and
honour love.

CHAPTER 6

It's a Love Thing

It seemed like a school assembly as I sat amongst the seven elders,
And the main speaker had now taken the platform.
"I am Love, and through Wisdom, I become your furnished table,
Surrounded here by elders.
And beautifully displayed with the best foods that you can think of,
Including champagnes and red wines, and not to mention
The overflowing of best spring waters you can find."

Now what would you say
If I told you that such a feast really does exist?
And the main presence awaits you?
Because this table has been set especially for you.
What if I told you another secret: that if you were really hungry
And knew that this beautiful setting was much nearer to you than
breath,
would you walk away? Or gladly partake?
Had it not been for the illusionary wall that you erected,
That has now made you believe you just can't step right in.

I am the chandeliers in the ceiling, giving you light for a new meaning
as you dig in.
I am the picture on the wall; you make a comment just to initiate
conversation,

As though if you were to stay silent, you could no longer remain here.
Since you could not sustain your brain, much less bear your pain,
And by that you would certainly perish. But I beckoned you unto myself,
Even through the side of the wall that you built.
Of course, not that I could not eradicate the trace withal,
But how would you be able to identify your witness
Who has become your point of reference as you choose heaven or hell?
Now can you see that without me, you really would cease to exist?
Without you, I too, would cease to exist.

I am all the ingredients put together, in creating this lovely cake you see.
Including your watering mouth and the sounds as you uttered, "Yes, please."
I am the touch that you feel as it crumbles at your fingertips.
Look at those shades, colours, and designs,
Stimulating with delight all those taste buds,
Ready to capture what's not yet in your mouth.
And as you raise me up to your nose, so wonderful, the aroma,
You can't help but to close your eyes to the heavens,
And with one bite, you realise heaven is really there,
Without having the need to ask, exactly where.
But with the elation of that realisation,
You discover through that insight that you are really a part of me.

Love is the capsule whose ingredients consist of all the elders:
Faith that assures us of Presence, with Truth, Unity,
And to also be with Conviction and Endurance,
To overcome all trials through Forgiveness and to gain peace,
For piece of Love is what we ultimately seek,
Which becomes our eternal bliss.

Love is the kingdom in which all the elders exist;
That consist of the throne of kings and queens.
Whilst Love embraces and also rocks the crib of the newly born babe.

It is Love that whispers, "Bless you," and utters from the heart, "How do you do?"
She is from whence all things came and all things continue to reign.
Love is the entwinement of the cords that bind,
Including the shapes, contours, colours of the whole human race,
That says, "Whether black, brown, white, or yellow, you are mine."
Yet with that knowing, Love is never conceited, nor is she blind.
And just because Love is not self-seeking doesn't mean she is small.

Love is the capsule that you swallow,
Although you may have just wallowed,
But certainly does not leave you feeling hollow.
Because Love is the umbrella that shields
And also heals all living things
From all sorts of infectious dis-eases.
This is the reason that you have been prescribed
A universal dosage so divine, which anyone can exceed,
And to be administered through any sensory modality,
But orally taken, like a kiss, it gets quickly absorbed.
By that, you may not even have a need to pray.
Some may endure withdrawal symptoms
But guarantee no complaints about side-effects.

Sometimes intense, with Love, you will find heart-wrenching moments
So hard to define, but even in the midst of it all,
Love beckons you just "be still, for I am the Crimson Light within.
I am here to help, if you please."
Love is not boastful, nor competitive,
For what is there to be compared with?

Love said, "Apart those of the elders, I'm often called by many other names.
Some say I am the open heart and basic kindness, of giving and receiving;
A gift: as Christ spirited me, and others say I am ultimate goodness in every way.
Love is the Omnipotent and Omniscient Presence."
But whatever name you choose, Love doesn't mind
Or complain, because she understands
The language of every heart, including their game plan.
But Love simply says, "I am that, I am.
Whatever you want me to be, that I am!

"My characteristics are universally the same;
Because irrespective of race, gender, or cultural practices,
You could all find me in yourselves.
Note: Wherever you are in the world,
You cry and laugh and hurt the same,
Hence, my ultimate goal is to bring you unto myself
That where I am, there you may be also."

To Love, we are all equal as one, because the blessing of gifts
Love never fails to bestow and is delivered to all on time.
It is often said, "Love makes you blind."
Love says, "I know that you may find this strange,
But this happens only when one chooses to stay in the waiting game.
Be very conscious, for this I say: I have come that the blind might see."

The truth to be seen in transparent-seas;
Love exposes and reveals that which you must see,
Justice in all principalities,
To lead each one from bondage and to experience liberation.
"It is true that I am not a bed of roses; I am all the flowers and more."

However, when you get pricked by the thorns,
Just remember to focus your gaze
On the sweet-scented petals that leave a lasting trail.

I am the match stroked to your log as you set it aflame,
And there you will see that without you, my flame does not exist,
and vice versa.
Love is the "becoming" in Unity and recognition of every elder that
we meet,
And by her Presence, we are healed,
As we discover that even the shortcuts of Forgiveness
Also guarantee success.
However, love still reminds us that the virtue we often seek
Is actually in the journey of our quest.

Love is becoming aware
That to actualise self-full love through the Crimson Light,
Is the realisation you are, indeed, light.
As the sweetness of the marrow holds the dose of healing in the bone,
So is Love onto all there is, the constant light that glows within.
It is the acceptance of self and that of the other:
Sister or brother; group or community; country or continent.
And when administered with Presence, Love becomes certainly felt.

Love offers freedom to all who will hear
And ensures the whispers in their heart: "I love you, dear."
By the illusion of her lack, many write sad songs: "I Want You Back,"
Because they had failed to follow instructions that she calls all to
obey.
Do you feel entrapped? Because Love will unbind you,
Since Love is victorious in all life's deeds.
Are you willing to partake of her sweetness
That she willingly and abundantly displays?

Love synchronises and harmonises, in bringing you unto her bosom;
A safe haven has been assured: including Final Destination Resort.
Open and sharing Love attracts and simply subtracts what is not divine,
By that you come to know that which really is,
And even though she may seem intricate, Love simplifies
Enacting, arranging, mobilising
Transcendental energy. Love is strong.

You say to yourself, "I am working with Conviction
To live with Faith and Unity and to exhibit Truth,
And that's why I am learning Forgiveness,
So that I can fully experience being with Presence."
But I say, the next time you meet the little old lady
Who says to you, "Hello Love,"
You had better hold her in high esteem.

Love explained, "Knowing who you are is important,
Because I cannot see myself in myself,
And that is why I reflect myself through you, as mirrors;
By that you learn through the Open University of Life
How to gain your achievement of loving thyself with honours
And avoid the long dreaded process like Fear."
At this stage, Love proceeded to tell me about the guy name Fear,
Whom, of course, I had met several times (perhaps even one too many).

According to Love, like the other elders, Fear had completed the self-full love programme with distinction. However, shortly after enrolling in the course for Mastership Love Programme, Fear dropped out and, of course, found himself immediately broken. Thus having been removed from the whole group, he inevitably created a curse on himself.

Fear became so angry that he turned red hot and instantly panicked because he was faced with having to pursue something that he had not planned for: working with strange people at the primary level in GPS. Because he showed them so many things that they would not have otherwise known, they simply adored him.

Missing the other elders like he did, Fear concluded that he had short-changed himself and consequently drowned himself in a bottle of spirits. The panic attacks increased at each thought: Now, I am no longer seen as the bright and illuminating one. A snowball effect evolved as he embarked on new ventures which, invariably, resulted in frequent severe attacks.

Being very charismatic, Fear arrogantly thought that he could get back on course, just like that. It was not that simple. He would have to apply for sponsorship, granted through Love, and was also required to develop true character-building, like having the ability to be patient, for example. Being impatient, he concluded that the reason for the delayed response to his application was that it had been denied.

Feeling rather stupid each time he tried making something new happen, he'd say, "I, Fear, have made a real mess of things." In essence, he had missed the creative minds of the other elders. For this reason, he continued reaffirming to himself over and over: "I, Fear, have been rather stupid!" He became fearful even of his own self, which meant he also found himself on edge and created endless havoc. Naturally, he blamed everyone and everything for his damn foolishness."

According to Love, "That is exactly what happens when you feel stupid: You can't think straight. Fear developed what is commonly known as schizophrenia, a multiple personality disorder."

On hearing this, I was hoping that my "three selves" business was not going to be categorised as such. However, Love said that the elders looked down on Fear, and they saw that it was just too hot for him. Therefore, they held a conference and decided to intervene, as it seemed like Fear was actually crying out for help. They decided to get to the bottom of the issue with Unity. An interview was arranged with Unity, hoping to determine what Fear was seeking.

Unity: "Fear, where are you going?"
Fear: "Going to and fro."
Unity: "Doing what?"
Fear: "Seeking whom I may devour."

Of course, Fear knew very well being on heat, like he was, meant a lot of damage had been done. People had gotten burnt because Fear, filled with spirit, moves really fast and that, in turn, ignites into red flames.

It turned out, Fear was scared he might not have been able to prove his competence in achieving a good grade on the Mastership Love Programme, especially since he felt that he was the brightest of them all.

He kept repeating, "You see, I, Fear, have made a real mess of things. I seem to have lost my head." The repetitions of his pitiful statements caused Unity to feel sad for him, played in her head as a jingle, by which a seed had been sewn that enabled her to understand Fear.

Later, Unity reported back to the other elders: "I saw that all a person's thoughts evolve like seeds in the ground, ready to burst. Look at it this way: If all a person's thoughts and actions are like seeds that become rooted and bear fruits after their kind, then clearly, Fear's action to break away from us was not a healthy seed to sow in the world."

"The truth of the matter is, since Fear had broken off course and saw himself as a curse, the next thing followed: He was faced with the need for a cure. For this reason, I want us to encourage others to think good thoughts for healthy seeds. This way, we can create a strong bond in the world. I want you all to get what I am saying".

Unity continued, "Therefore, we must remember that 'O' represents the circle that we are all part of, whether it is perceived as good or evil: but nevertheless, whole. Like the picture of a child screaming with arms stretched out wide, naturally, Fear took on the shape of the weakest link, 'C' devastatingly seeking its counterpart, that mirrors and attracts another 'C.' As the two merge and face each other, they become whole and may even form a strong bond in the world. The trouble is, not unless one first takes an objective view as though she were the child with the claps of the hands, palms facing each other, which takes the form the whole, will he continue to experience being the link, seeking its counterpart."

Therefore, it is vital that to be whole, one ought to see himself as such: whole. This, however, in my experience of being faced with Fear, can only be gained through Love. If I should go with my gut feeling, we all need to be immunised with Love so that we can help others deal with Fear; otherwise, we won't be able to go back down there, and what use would we be then? Said Unity.

Love added, "Sad, to think one actually allows himself to be so petrified of his ability to do good that he opts out of the game, hoping to avoid shame; now that's so insane."

When I heard this, I thought, But that's exactly what had happened to me. I felt that I would not be good enough.

In 1973, the annual Secondary School Magazine published one of my stories. With little concern as to whether my story would even be published, I just submitted it and forgot about it. So I was amazed that I had been recognised for my achievement by my peers. Nevertheless, my joy quickly subsided by what seemed like everyone pressuring me about my next story, asking what it would be about. And was it going to be as good as the first? And on hearing that, I panicked. I felt an obligation to escape the ransom that I had to hit the same mark or do even better. I was not willing to risk disappointing all those people with such high expectations of me.

According to Love, Unity along with Conviction was with Fear for a second time. Their compassion intensified Fear's desire to reunite with the other elders. Thereafter, Fear became an expert at breaking all kinds of bolts and locks, safes and vaults; no matter what the combination, he did them all, just to get back on course. Fear not only enrolled in the Mastership Programme, he succeeded in the following courses: Wisdom, Healing, Prophesy, Knowledge, Faith, Miracles, and Languages.

Love said, "Fear devoured all the units, just like that."

"How was he able to do that?" I asked.

"It's called 'transference skills,' in which he applied himself through four dimensions. The other elders, on the other hand, operated on only three dimensions: Decision, Discipline, and Determination, with the exception of Discernment: a unit that could only be attained from the Open University of Life and serves as a bridge (or the ability to make dicisions) to Actualising Self-full Love and to recognise one's chosen gift."

As I listened, I could not help but think, I must have learnt something of that D-factor from Fear, since everything Love had related seemed clear. Love said Fear also had to overcome his embarrassment of facing each of the elders, who turned out to be very supportive of him. One could say that his intention to return home to his friends had become the turning point of the prodigal son, who had acknowledged his foolishness to his father, after squandering his inheritance. Fear had processed the feeling of his abandonment of pride, guilt, and shame, and the anticipation of embracing the domain of wholeness once again.

Fear had formed a legacy of one removing the sandals off her feet, so to speak, for the ground which she stands upon is holy. It was the recognition of his containment that he needed to become one with the Crimson Light. You could say that Fear had become the demarcation of transformation as the offer of bullocks at the altar and the restoration of peace and harmony, including the freedom from strife and the clapping hands that embrace all blissful gains. Basically, Fear is coarse salt, biblically labelled as Lot's wife, waiting to be processed as granules or refined in order that it can be defined in whatever and wherever it is.

According to Love, the most wonderful thing that happened throughout the Master's Programme was that Fear developed a clear understanding of the spirit of Discernment. This was the only module that could allow him to make the distinction from where he was and where he wanted to be. It was the merging of two worlds. Hence, it was not necessary for the other elders, since they in turn represented the brother of the prodigal son; they stayed home on the Bridge of Actualising Self-full Love. Notwithstanding, Discernment has since been a mandatory unit to the Master's Programme.

According to Love, although Fear knew how to reassimilate himself with the elders, he was nevertheless unaware that he had to face the naked Truth to submit his application with Resignation, so that he could be with Forgiveness. That was Fear's biggest challenge ever, to be with Forgiveness, and for this reason, he needed Faith. He discovered that the longer it took him to accept Truth, the worse he felt. That, in turn, became the seed for procrastination: the flip side of being on course. Basically, Fear now served as a checkpoint for all intentions.

Having listened to Love up until that point, I felt empathy for Fear because then, it made sense why Christ endorsed the idea to always be with Forgiveness. For this is how you not only win friends, but you stand to influence people and situations, as well.

According to Love, it is important that we remember that Fear can only affect us by finding something like him in us to attach himself to. Therefore, it's easy to acknowledge him, just as long as we can identify what that something is and take responsibility for our actions.

Think of Fear as a form of circumcision, the cutoff point, which indicates something is no longer necessary, or even a signature on the dotted line. It's a point of the inner calling of your heart strings, which requires you to trust the driving force of the Crimson Light. Thus, having Faith to believe in the promise of Presence and to have Conviction, even though tempted to wish it were not so. Love also said that we must have Wisdom to know exactly what is required to work with Endurance in upholding the pangs of pain that often cause the heart to ache and the knees to shake. However, once you have consented with Resignation and with the spirit of Unity, which merges and bonds, you then becomes whole.

According to Love, if you look well, you will be able to tell that Fear's role in this sphere is really playing the clown, directing individuals, groups, and countries out of the hell game and into Love. That is why you'd often hear him say, "Been there, done that, and even got a T-shirt to prove it."

Now, my understanding is that a lot of trouble lies with students of primary and secondary level; they just love identifying themselves with the T-shirts. I think it's all to do with those prints. The thing is, people just need to find a way to motivate the students: by pivoting their attention away from plagiarising, polarising, and prioritising the T-shirt as a product. Then, they can assimilate themselves by producing a profitable profile for their divine intended profession. Now that's why I am careful of what labels and writings I wear.

Love said that Fear gained his master's degree with distinction. The other elders were so fascinated by his achievements that they nominated him as head principal of the Open University of Life, which specialises in how to find Love. Hence the reason, after being on course, all Fear's students graduate and eventually retire in Love and claim to feel on top of the world.

It is said that Fear always begins his lectures with these ten words: "Fear no one, for I have come to reign supreme."

It takes the students awhile to get it, but after they have repeated the mantra so many times, they become amazed of the realisation of their personal transformation on a higher plane because by then, they are no longer with Fear.

The sad thing that I have also come to understand is that Fear has had a very hard time trying to convince people that he is indeed the flip side of the coin, working harmoniously with Love for the good of all humankind. It's like your hair has always been considered glory but does this mean that your toenails don't belong to the body just the same? Hence the reason why Love felt it necessary to announce, "I have not given you the spirit of Fear, but of sound mind."

If only we believe Fear actually serves us well by pushing us to the edge, so that we can actually fall until death do us part: the dying of that which must take place to experience Love, on the other side of the coin, just like shedding limiting beliefs reminds us that we can no longer hide, for a new life awaits us through the Crimson Light.

I was amazed that Love had actually spent such a long time just talking about Fear, whom I previously had been trying to forget. But actually, the more I heard about Fear, the more I developed an appreciation for him. Now I understand why certain people actually get motivated by Fear.

With that, I concluded that it must have been through Love that everything was strategically put in place, and that I was always exactly where I needed to be, doing exactly what I was doing, at the exact time: to Actualising Self-full Love.

I felt that my journey has been just like Wilde said, that desire was indeed the inception to attaining my goal. There I was with a sense of wholeness because all my needs had been provided at each step on the way to getting onto the Bridge of Actualising Self-full Love.

Then I saw that it was necessary to provide me with Fear's story, so that I would have both an internal and external representation of how I had followed down the familiar pattern of a "C." That, in effect, became the link I intermittently anchored onto and eventually found my cure.

I ended my summary, and the elders seemed to be flowing at random.

"Well done, good and faithful servant; in you I am well pleased," said Love. "You have indeed passed your test."

My cheeks felt as though they had gone beyond their elasticity and came back as pillars. "I am very happy to be on here, on this bridge," I responded.

"Tests are not a requirement for here; we understand it not only serves as a point of reference for yourself but is also considered necessary for others to witness and to learn. For example, you made the choice to accept the loss of the diary: your best report, as you put it, and then retreated into stillness. Often, this is how people are able to motivate and nominate themselves and others by increasing their sense of awareness and gain awards that depict the evolution of humankind.

"Medals and trophies of adoration are not always available to the naked eye but are meant to serve as reminders of advancements to fuel one's life journey of Actualising Love."

"Likewise, bear this in mind," Truth said. "There are no brothers, no sisters, no cousins, no uncles, no aunts, no mothers, no fathers, no friends, no foes but all one in spirit. These units only serve as points of reference, by which you understand that I, Love, have presented you as gifts onto myself, that I am in the midst of all. Furthermore, this is never to impress us because we already know your every outcome, even before its inception."

"Well done to have held on so close to the bunch of keys," said Endurance, "even though there were times you thought that Faith had failed."

"Uh huh!" Faith exclaimed. "I was never going to fail you; in any case, I am not in the business of failing, period. You just had to go through the process to understand that it is she who endures to the end, she who stays in the wining game with Endurance."

And then, they read before me the first verse of Isaiah 60: "Arise, shine; for thy light is come and the glory of the Lord is risen upon thee." On hearing those words, I felt as though a strong cord had strung up seven pillars inside of me: three supporting me on either side, and the other shot straight from the top of my head to the base of my spine.

And as though reading my mind, Conviction asked, "Any questions you'd like to ask?"

"Yes, it's still about the bunch of keys that I discovered in GPS. What did they mean?"

"Oh, haven't you guessed? The answer that you seek is right there in your breath."

I said, "Do you mean life?"

"Yes, the keys represent us, the seven elders, aiding all on their journey in the Open University of Life."

Just as I had guessed, I thought.

He said, "Keys give you access to what lies not only ahead but also beyond, by which one gains access to knowing oneself at a deeper level.

The elders marvelled at the fact that I still held onto the keys; they would stay with me until I reached the Bridge.

"But why silver?" I asked.

Conviction replied, "Silver denotes spirit, as well as infinity, often referred to as 'source.'"

Then I remembered how we had worn gray at Mr Altidore's descent and concluded, "Perhaps this means that the elders are really spirits.

"What of the tombed casket" I asked.

"Well, no doubt, in time, I'm pretty sure you'd work it out," said Endurance. "However, since you asked, now it's all about making everything light. For example, St Lucians, like many others around the world, are waking up to the awareness of energy that I Am. A representation of death with the flip side of that 'I Am.' For instance, now that you have shed yourself of old, deeply seated unhealthy habits that weighed you down, you are bound to feel light. Therefore, when you motivate others through your action, by developing healthy life plans, you'll know for sure it is achievable."

"Setting up good values," Conviction began, "for the highest good of all concerned, is our universal goal. Therefore, people would consume fewer carcasses that in the end make their corpse stink. No longer will there be a need for the long dreary process of decaying for the return of dust. Thus, keeping in mind that the soul returns home and the dust to be for the sowing of seeds, a flower or a tree, it must conceive that which is evermore."

Now, I was really convinced that like life, death can be a beautiful poem.

Then that drew me to ask, "What about Mr Altidore? Did he really die?"

"Well, remember, there is no death."

"I mean the end of his passing breath," I said.

"Well, yes. Tell me how else would you have known that the weight you had carried just had to be offloaded? Hence, the road you now tarry on is light. Did you not notice the sign on the bridge? 'No load beyond this point'; the 'soul' requirement is only your boarding pass because I, Love, I am light."

The elders told me that the load I had carried was not just my own but also of generations gone by. "Is that not unfair?" I asked.

"Nothing is fair or unfair; how do you think you have come to be here? Many have had the passing of their breath that you, too, might live. From the cup that you drink, the sushi foods you eat, the Boteng clothes you wear, and including the Figaro that you drive, remember: Someone had the passing of their breath that you, too, might live."

"What if you never drive or even take a ride in a car?"

"In which case, my dear child, don't you ever wonder about those who designed and made your shoes? For everything that you see, just remember, it is not about being fair but, in true essence, it is to hold each other dear.

"Take a look around as you wake up in the morning; from the bed you slept upon, to the window that you opened, to the roof over your head, to the toothbrush that you handle (including the paste of your choice). Tea or coffee, as you reach on the shelf, black or white, instant or percolated, heated via electric or gas or even charcoal, served on porcelain or earthware (since you have given up drinking from the calabash), stirred with fine cutlery as you decide one or two sugars, just so that you can effortlessly enjoy a cup of tea today."

"Remember, many have had their passing breath so you, too, might live," Presence.

In addition, I was directed to the proverb "In all labour there is profit." They explained that as an example, GPS had gained substantially from a trust that was set up in the name of Finding Your Voice by Mr Barack Altidore: "It is for this reason each child of GPS had to endure a graze that would brook with pain. The course serves as a necessary prerequisite for their adaptation, in the Open University of Life. Thus, the impact of the graze would present a choice to seek further education. In a roundabout way, students find themselves going back in time in order to make sense of their world."

"Now, Hope for the People, of course, is where you conform to the choices you make," said Forgiveness, "and that does not have to be any specific establishment, per se, but rather, it's the state of the decision you make. For instance, whether to be healed on this plane or to transcend through your Final Destination Resort: the demarcation to enter into another realm, thereby returning to the source. That is indeed Hope for the People."

Though tempted to refer to him as Dirty Harry, I asked Love about Mr Altidore's assistant; he replied, "He is an angel. Angels are there to assist whenever they are called upon. They're all around you."
I smiled because I felt Love right there and then.

I proceeded to enquire about the cornfield, but like Chatterbox, not waiting for a response, I said, "I believe it meant that whatever I would discover would be like an eternal abundance of good food: Like the essence of living orderly; it presented the outcome of ideas as grains sown into the ground. Each stalk signified strength as the constant winds blew over their heads."

Now I declared my barns are filled and overpouring is a promise fulfilled. Instead of a sack of guilty charges, I saw that I can now have an everlasting supper, not only with the elders but the whole world, with Love.

"My child, you have certainly learned well. Just keep on keeping on," Love said.

And as a reminder of my mission statement with determination, I felt both statements had served me well.

"Love, you have been kind and gracious," I said. "I thank you, but can you please explain to me about Christian, the other observer?"

"We knew that you had been pursuing how to know me, so we ensured that Christian would serve as a signpost on your journey. His presence would no doubt alert your attention because of his serious and self-disciplined nature, which you secretly admired, of course.

"We also anticipated your choice to review those moments with Christian that coincided with the challenges you endured through your son and came close to giving up. Now you, too, can see why Christian had to be there."

Then Forgiveness said, "We were happy to discover that though you really knew it was Christian standing there, after a short while, you did not care. Most importantly, this was to offer you an opportunity to release yourself of shame and blame, which you once found hard to release."

"Thank you," I said. "Speaking of release, what about my inner spilling of the beans, with all those confessions?"

Love said, "How else would you have learnt to receive your ease and contribute to the world of transparent-seas? The Crimson Light shining through your soul, its purpose here must be told, for others, including yourself, will become elders and not lost in dismay." And with an earnest look, Love continued, "I've been seeking various ways through humankind's willingness just to express myself. Therefore, I have extended myself as diversities of gifts of various talents to each individual. By their operation, you will come to know that I am not in just some of you, but indeed, I am in every one of you. Like, there are many members working together in one body, so you are all one spirit, working in one body through the Crimson Light. Then, I understood that we are asked to love one another, even for our own good."

"Tell me about Mrs Blanchard's look-alike, I mean the woman in black."

"She is your earthly guardian angel," said Unity. "She understands the diverse spoken and unspoken language of all forms of life and demonstrates the willingness to serve individuals, communities, and even countries, just to show that we are all one."

"Notice when you were experiencing pain and shame, the people around you often got blamed, and they, too, perhaps ended up feeling the same. Now that you are experiencing life-changing lanes, leaving your trail of overflowing gains, people around will undoubtedly want to play your game or even change their life lanes. That's what happens when you have been on the Bridge to Actualising Self-full Love. Once here, and spirit-filled granted with Love, you will certainly find great peace of mind; by that, you will also have fun because you won't easily break down" said Truth.

Then Love said, "As people progress towards Actualising Self-full Love, the inevitable transformation will make them become lighter not only in themselves, but in the execution of their projects. Think about it: lighter bodies of illumination, gained through purposeful meditation and mindfulness, including less consumption of flesh; when you are gone and your body laid down to rest, there won't be much of a stench. Mr Barack Altidore was not only light in mind but also in body and spirit; hence, you can't say for sure whether he'd actually gone down or up. Or could it have been that you were positioned upside down? Perhaps a choice you had unconsciously made in how you wish to view the world? As you have learned from the Emerald Tablet, circa 3000 BC: "As above, so below. As within, so without." So I ask you: Did Mr Altidore actually descend or ascend"?

Perhaps such a question can only be resolved by further stillness, I thought.

Love continued, "Look into my eyes; what do you see? Am I not the one you saw stepping in what you termed the tombed casket, just like that? Am I not the warm glow that hovered over your head and the voice between your ears?

"I am that bond between the acts, and your perception,
Though often obscured, you still manage to find new meaning.
Remember, I am the energy in life's chameleon dancing cycle,
That guided you onto the Bridge of Actualising Self-full Love."

Then, Love asked whether I had anything else to say before allowing me to roam. Being on such a high with Love, I decided to summarise my feelings:

"Ah! I am so grateful and thankful that I feel completely healed. Now I really understand why it is said that you shouldn't judge a book by its cover. What I had seen, with Mr Altidore stepping into the tombed casket, just like that, has now totally transformed me. For this reason, I will continue to live by Faith and Unity, ensuring to be with Forgiveness so that I have Conviction to live with Presence. And to also accept that Truth dwells within me, so I can use Endurance to succeed in becoming the person I am born to be: free to roam on the Bridge of Actualising Self-full Love.

Anchoring Points

There are no accidents and no coincidences, but the choices we make:
Today, I am making a choice to see
life through the eyes of the creator,
life as beautiful, and
life through the Crimson Light.

I am now open and receptive to the guidance of the Crimson Light;
therefore, I am trusting the choice I have made to
accept life as a gift,
embrace the polarities, and
bless everything arround me.

The Diversity of the Gifts

"Now ... I would not have you ignorant about the diversity of gifts; but the same spirit. And there are differences of administrations, but the same Lord. And there are diversities of operations, but it is the same God who worketh all in all. But the manifestation of the Spirit is given to every man to profit withal. For to one is given by the Spirit the word of wisdom ... to another knowledge ... to another Faith ... to another gifts of Healing ... to another Miracles ... to another Prophesy ... and to another discerning of the spirits ... to another Language; including divers kinds of tongues and interpretation of tongues. For by one spirit we are all baptised into one body." Corinthians Chapter twelve verses four to twelve (12: V 4-12).

Who shall find a virtuous woman?
For her price is far more than rubies.
She consders a field and buys it...
With the fruits of hands she plants a vineyard.
She girds her loins with strength and make her arms strong.
She perceives that her merchandise is good.
Her clothing is silk and purple.
Her husband is known in the gates when he sits among the elders...
Strength and honour are her clothing:
And she shall rejoice in time to come.
She open her mouth with wisdon
And in her tongue is the law of kindness.

Proverbs chaper 31

CHAPTER 7

Why Are You Here?

Now if anyone should ask me 'why are you here?' The answer would be clear "to serve and be served." To serve Just like Iyanla Vanzant and many others; as having got my back, I've got yours too. Now, I know for sure, that to serve and to be served, are really one and the same; just flip side of the same coin: a coin that consists not only the substance required for getting onto the Bridge of Actualising Self-full Love, but it allows one to see themselves as who they really are.

What did I hear? I heard, Mr Barack Altidore just as before, saying "I just want the bloody combination for this thing!" Nothing more, nothing less. Now, I say to you, one and all, consider yourselves worthy! Because now, as a witness, you too, have the "bloody combination"; and that's definitely no more a secret.

What did I touch? Not quite sure, but through the spirit of Endurance, it felt like I had touched the left side of Denzel Washington's chest. And though it is said that it's in the heart that you'll find all manner of evil reigns, I also know, it's also the place, after one has fallen, where there is always the chance to rise up again in love. For where you find one, there too, you shall find the other; just the flip side of the same coin.

What did I smell? The flowers in Oprah's back yard; but wait a minute. I have the same right here, and even in full bloom with the sweet fragrance of pure White Linen.

What did I taste? The fusion of tropical fruits made in heaven and simply out of this world, whilst packed with sweet words of wisdom. Thus, the prophecy to heal the world would be fulfilled and would not return void.

What did I see? Well, I saw the most wonderful and amazing sight of everyone forming an "O," but I don't just mean like that of The Oprah Winfrey Show. I could also see, though not with my naked eyes, but somehow I could see, undeniably without a doubt, one huge universal everlasting "O." One synchronising with the essence of each individual's soul, as an acknowledgement of their OWN' uniqueness, yet embracing the words of the host of the show: "We are more alike than we are different!"

Ah! But as I leisurely looked around, the other thing I saw was a little Oprah right in front of me, with a tear rolling from her eye, yet with a smile. And there over to my back was the feeling of two little hands pushing and the most familiar voice of Iyanla saying, "I've got your back. I've got your back."

Now look over the bus stop to my right; there's Deepak! Is he really driving that bus? Anyway, you can trust him to guide you to your intended destination or even show you how to know God.

"Cooking a real gourmet tonight?" the cashier asked, as she rang up my bill.

Ah! There's Maya! Singing and swinging tonight, I guess.

Well, there's no mistake there, I'd just gone on to sign up at the gym, when I thought, It must be my head.

"Quick," I said. "Get Djehuty from the health store; God knows I do not want to go insane."

Then I realised I was still on the Bridge of Actualising Self-ful Love. Phew! It was really him! The placid Denzel guy, I mean.

He just looked at me and smiled, and that had me blushing for a while. Then, Louise asked emphatically, "Who cares?"

Just remember to be gentle with yourself, for it is from the outpouring of your heart that you truly get to know what has been kept inside. Of course, just remember, none of this is ever without your consent.

Why are you here? Just roaming to and fro, I thought. The question that had seemed to come from nowhere had prompted a need to summarise my journey and consequently left me with the beginning of another confession. However, it anchored on the premise "I will leave no stone unturned."

Without any inclination to disguise, I opened my mouth. "I have been going to bed with two that I had mentioned at the onset of my journey," I said, "one named Paul and the other Dick. Might I just say, only one at a time. However, they seemed like elders, too. Please don't ask me which one of the men I like best, because they are both brilliant at making me feel good. Paul certainly touches every part of me, as he gets me to completely relax by the gentle rise and fall that happens all by itself, and then I just let go. He is also quite resourceful, with a wide range of techniques which he uses for stimulating all my senses and for helping me achieve my desired outcomes. Now, when it comes to changing position, I just revert to his course and change my life in seven days: a job well done, and then, I'm good to go.

"On the other hand, I really like Dick. Perhaps it's the way he'd say, 'Feel your thighs and hips relaxing, one part at a time. In fact, I imagined that this was exactly how Mr Barack Altidore's voice had sounded. With Dick, I'm never too tired to employ him."

One could say that the law of Attraction was in motion, as both men displayed so much in common. As often said, birds of a feather flock together, and that's exactly how we were. As it happened, I found out that they were using the same techniques on me: hypnotising me with their seductive words. Naturally, they would have their way with me, and that would be it. However, I tried my technique for both men: one at a time, of course, and that was in pursuit of my quest: Why am I here? Both times, I chose not to go under, so to speak. Instead, I remained awake, only to discover that they really meant me well. What could I say but "Carry on, carry on."

To keep my men, we came up with a plan, and this time there would be no messing around. We'd be a family, but we needed to build our house. I was reminded by Paul to always start with the end goal in mind. For example, what do we want our house to look like, be like, and feel like? The vision had become my mission.

"Become a virtuous woman and attain wisdom" had been my prayer; and I was ready to explore its manifestation in all my operations. So I thought of what the wisest man, Solomon, the son of King David, said about building a house. I took a glance into his words of wisdom, and right there in the manual of life, the Holy Bible, this is what I saw: "Wisdom has hewn her house on seven pillars." What could that mean? I could not comprehend what the seven pillars were. However, I reaffirmed my belief, in a loud exclamation: "I, Lauviah, will know what I need to know at the right time, space, and sequence."

My men, on the other hand, often complimented me, even at my every action and intention. I found Dick to be totally accepting of me, as he'd often say, "You are fine just as you are," and that, of course, directed my attention to become more accepting of myself. As they continued to touch every cell of my being with their words, my imagination would run wild. I increasingly developed behaviours that confirmed that whatever they had spoken was true.

"Come, I'll sing you a song, and we can dance all night long," said Dick. I felt a gentle kiss to my lips, a taste so divine.

"You smell so sweet and so hard to resist," Paul said.

But once again, I had allowed my imagination to run away with me. You see, I was really ready to see who I was because that would mean I will know why I am here, I thought.

It was through my reflection on Chatterbox I realised that I always had the air of Presence, even though I was often misunderstood. And I felt so strong, and my confidence way high. I saw that I am a loving and creative woman with imagination backpacked by my acts of faith and to make my dream a reality, even though I had been with Fear. Being with the elders mirrored my virtues to perfection. I felt truly worthy of my wish to conceive.

"Good news," said my men, "since our purpose is to be fruitful, multiply, replenish, and subdue the earth."

With acknowledgements of our delight, Dick asked, "shall we dance?"

Well, since I was already in high heels that I had gotten from Louise, with Resignation, I gladly said, "Yes, please."

Eagerly we went to sleep, trying night after night, week after week, and month after month to conceive. Nothing happened. After feeling despair, I prayed for the power of the Crimson Light to perform a miracle, to have my baby. Then, I would proclaim to the world that the Crimson Light, thus, reigned in me. After all, I still held the belief that all things are possible, and so with Faith, I reminded myself that my whole journey had been a miracle anyway. Therefore, I was able to appreciate the space and resources like the vision board, prayers, and affirmations in terms of what my life would look like. I was playing my mind movies over and over, several times daily, in preparation of our intention.

Yet something seemed amiss. I will confess that I even retrieved on of Stuart Wilde's movie: another man who not only taught me about self-discipline and self-respect, he also tickled my fancy.

By the time I was done with the tick tock in my mind, you could hear me singing aloud, "Wilde thing, you make my heart sing; you make everything Wilde. Wilde thing, I think I love you! DA! DA! DA! DA!"

I expected that I had naturally transferred this high energy into my men, who had not ceased to perform well; it just seemed to take so long to conceive.

> True power comes through cooperation and silence.
> —Ashanti proverb

Therefore, I retreated further into stillness and solitude, which had me reflecting on all I needed to do, and who and what I needed to forgive, or what residue of restrictions I might have been holding. Nothing! Because I felt free and healed in my body, mind, and spirit, so I continued to hold onto Faith.

The woman in black was crystal clear about the prophecy she had shared: "Once you are healed, no longer will you remain barren, because you are the mother of many sons," and this I believed in my heart.

In honour of what I believed to be real, I began to sing, "I believe in miracles" with my whole being, and immediately, I felt a deep sense of Presence permeating all my separate selves. From there on, I was able to see that what I was looking for was right there within me: The Crimson Light inside had enabled me to assimilate myself with the elders, who had been with me from the primary level. They had helped me on my journey, and that, in essence, was through Love. I had found something like myself in them, on which I could attach myself to them.

The elders had transformed into Mr Altidore, Chatterbox, Resignation, Christian, Harry, Fear, and of course, the woman in black. Each had merged through the four general stages of learning:

primary, secondary, further education, and higher education. As graduates, they were transformed as Faith, Forgiveness, Presence, Endurance, Conviction, Truth, and Unity.

By serving their purpose through the evolution of various guises, the elders would present their recipients the choice to flip sides of any situation. Only this time, I thought I was done with flipping sides when suddenly, like the sound of withdrawing money from an ATM machine, the pictures continued to download.

I was faced with pictures of Euyah and the elders. I saw that whilst Euyah's face had been the same on his seven passports, the elders each had different guises. Euyah's places of birth were from seven different countries, but the elder's origin was of the Crimson Light. This means their date of birth is universally timeless: often called "eternity." Why this revelation at this time? I wondered. I also saw how Harry, Mr Altidore's assistant, through his miraculous ability, could transform his fiery nature to melt down locks and bolts (including tombs or vaults). Thus, his red veil symbolised all bloody issues of birth and the need for survival, and this is how he gained Conviction.

Another flash of Mr Altidore and the tombed casket had resurfaced, as did the gut feeling that Conviction also possessed the key that would unlock my womb, as though it were a tomb. I knew it! Just like it had been before discovering Euyah's passports, I kept repeating, "Something's not right," until I blurted the words right out. Likewise, I had heard myself blurting out, "He who had the 'bloody combination' to the tombed casket is also he who has the 'bloody combination' to my womb!'" And that followed the words: "You've got to be willing to do the work."

But it was the voice of Djehuty that had influenced me, by these very words. As though feeling I was under some kind of test with Conviction, I discovered Djehuty, Harry, and Conviction were actually one and the same.

I was willing to do the work. And under the guise of Harry assisting Mr Altidore, I was faced with Djehuty asking me, "Why are you here?"

"To serve by being productive," I responded.

"As long as you are willing to do the maths, then you don't have a problem," he said. The transformation had taken place because mathematics was no longer my dreaded subject; quite the contrary, I was loving it.

"What would you say one and one does?" he asked.

"Create," I answered, because I was just thinking about my unborn baby.

"Right," he said.

I felt really good that I had answered correctly.

"Now what would you say is the basic principles for resolving any matter?"

"Add, subtract, divide, or multiply, for this is what it means to be fruitful, multiply, replenish, and subdue," I answered.
"Right!"

I felt elated by my discoveries as Djehuty continued his line of questioning.
"Since we want to increase, which of the four mathematical symbols should we use?"
I said, "Add or multiply."
"Okay, but what would guarantee a maximum increase of the sum?"
I replied, "Multiplication."

"Right," he said.

That was really primary level education, I thought. However, I remembered, life is a dance, and it may seem like you are going backward before you can move forward. Furthermore, to give up just like that would mean that you are really subtracting yourself out of the equation and, ultimately, your attendance at the Open University of Life. Plus, it really makes no sense to do that because you may just have to go through the whole process of enrolling again, like Fear.

Since Determination is my middle name, I reminded myself that I was going to see this through, to have my baby. I was feeling very good about myself and the continued support of my men. So with Faith, I repeated this affirmation several times: "I love and accept myself exactly as I am."

The fact that I was getting help had got me so excited, I began to dance. I danced as I did to the sounds that were forbidden as a child. I would knock onto the bottom of the pots with a spoon to create my own tune. I was now free to let go of myself, to raise my energy levels and express gratitude, for my expectancy to conceive.

Then Djehuty said, "Even as you dance, just remember: Everything, including our senses, are in direct relation to numbers. Everything."

Now when I heard this, I immediately sensed a small head with two bright eyes looking right at me, and a nose through which I felt a light breath against my face, and two earlobes with unique contours that resembled a "C." It also had a mouth that smiled at me. In addition, I noticed he had four limbs with ten fingers and ten toes. I saw lots of numbers.

My own senses seemed heightened by his sweet, soft, and silky skin, as though it had been brushed against blooming jasmine of fresh air. Since the numbers made me feel good and we were now adding up, I decided to do more maths.

I thought, Nothing happens by chance, but by choice. Nothing. So I went to work. Now, just like I had seen the number one quite a lot, this time I saw the numbers four and seven. They were everywhere. For this reason, I concluded it was not accidental that Euyah's passport, like the elders, were seven. They had attained seven gifts of the spirit, with veils that also corresponded to seven chakras, including seven colours of the rainbow and the number of trophies I had collected.

Then I also recalled that we were four, including Mr Barack Altidore, before his descent; four stages of the Mastership Love Programme, and I was now engaged in a desire that would involve four members of our family. In no time at all, I had mentally plonked the multiplication sign between the two numbers: four and seven, which equalled twenty-eight, and voila! Like I always say, "You have to do the maths." Was it a coincidence that twenty-eight happens to be the number of days in my menstrual cycle?

Anyway, right there and then, I had been shown the bloody combination to conceiving my baby; it was in the numbers. It was not by chance that I had heard Mr Altidore asking for the bloody combination. Could he have known that I would one day require the bloody combination for my womb? All I had to do next was figure out my ovulation period and keep my men happy; well, we'd all be happy.

As everything else breeds after its own kind, so also was my maths becoming good. Of course, the men and I immersed in countless symbols for the number seven: Seven days of the week and seven day of creation (that includes the day of rest); seven continents and the seven oceans; seven stars that guide us from ancient times; the seven objects visible in the cosmos: sun, moon, Mars, Mercury, Jupiter, Venus, and Saturn; seven digits for phone numbers (excluding area code); seven types of metal: tin, lead, copper, mercury, silver, gold, and zinc; and the seven different shapes: square, triangle, circle, rectangle, pentagon, heptagon, diamond. And there were more sevens. We also did the same with four, which represents the four mathematical formulae; the four forces of life: water, earth, wind, and fire; the four cardinal points; the four seasons of the year; the four gospels of the New Testament of Matthew, Mark, Luke, and John. Then, I saw perhaps there was a greater significance to why we were four at the event of Mr Altidore's departure.

Whatever happens in the heavens, so it is in the earth.

At this stage, Djehuty ensured me that there was nothing wrong with me. He said that the night I had slept in GPS had not been for just one hour, but that I had undergone seven hours of hypnotic therapy with Love. According to him, that was before I had looked at the clock on the wall that showed 11:00 p.m. (Of course, this made sense I had entered GPS in the afternoon time). Within those hours, they had performed a health check, which involved each elder attending to me for one hour. According to him, since there were no more lies and deceit in my heart, I was given the all-clear. Why did I have to confess then? It is because confession serve as a conscious demarcation of your will to evole.

"All you need now is a course of Moringa. It's a green herb that bears a long pod." He said that "a lot of men like the seeds, including Dick and Paul."

It is important to bear in mind that green is meant to help you focus on emotions of self-acceptance through Forgiveness. Therefore, there are going to be major change to your body. That's what Forgiveness does; she shifts things in order to create room for new. Then, I understood why Moringa is also referred to as the tree of life. What's more, it was also the secret behind Mr Altidore's miracle cure, which helped many St Lucians obtain a better lifestyle. As a result, nearly everyone now has a Moringa tree in their yard.

Djehuty explained that all my body required was to boost my immune system, and that would also regulate my menstrual cycle to perfection. Some things just have to be in place before another can be manifested; it is called "set principles of order." Then he drew on the analogy of a gardener turning the ground upside-down in preparation for producing a healthy plant. With my training on the farm of Mr All-Bags-Full, that is exactly what we did before we put the seed into the ground. And just like the tombed casket had accommodated Mr Barack Altidore, I was preparing my womb to accommodate my child.

My prescription had been to drink three cups of Moringa three times a day, for three days, and take one seed on the fourth day. Consequently, the ten intakes had coincided with the average ten- to nineteen-day ovulation of my menstrual cycle. Now that's what I call a course in miracles, because the Crimson Light had acknowledged my song and dance. However, when I think back, it seemed that my miracles began with the woman in black.

I was really ready to see myself through the wonderful elders that I met, especially to think that they must have found something like themselves in me, on which they could attach themselves to help me. Isn't that a wonderful thing? I thought.

We were ready to multiply after our kind.

It seemed as though a long multiplication had taken place, as an actual ascension in my womb, and the pregnancy test was announced: Positive! "Yes!" I exclaimed, without fear that I might have got it wrong. Positive was what I wanted, and negative was what I did not want. My wish had been granted, and shortly afterwards was the further confirmation of morning sickness. This time, I was not scared of what was inside me, because our baby had been conceived with love.

The process, I must admit, was quite intense, yet overall pleasantly exciting. We often danced to the sounds of conscious reggae and relaxed to soft jazz, which was the initial antidote for the contractions. The time for delivery had come. Dick was very quiet, whilst Paul, on the other hand, would not stop preaching: "See what you see; hear what you hear; and so on."

Thank God for the voice of Rick Clarke, I thought, as I breathed in deeply and exhaled fully.

After a few moments, Dick said, "You are fine just as you are."

Then I just pushed. All I know for sure is that there comes a time when you really must decide on what you feel is best for you. But to do that, you must first be ready to see who you are.

I saw that I am a mother, confirmed by the loud exclamation of the woman in black, who sang "Happy Birthday" to my son as he came out of my womb.

"Would you like to hold him?" she asked.

"What do you mean? Of course! Certainly," I responded.

Seeing the light through our baby's eyes was another revelation of the proverb, "In all labour, there is profit."

What would we name him? We had gone through a long list but changed our minds more than seven times, but nevertheless, we always maintained the belief that we would know what name to choose at the right time. He was just perfect. We were all simultaneously speaking the same words, when a sudden echo trailed across the room: "Enduranccccce." We were four, representing life's four elements, four pillars and everything else wonderful that four represents.

A most pleasing thing: I knew in my heart that my son's father and godfathers were happily supportive of us because they understood that they are indeed the fathers of many sons.

Shortly after, the elders reappeared and encircled us. One by one the elders laid their veils of rays over my head and reverently embraced us, and there was oneness on the Bridge of Actualising Self-full Love.

Anchoring Points

There are no accidents and no coincidences, but the choices we make:
Today, I am making a choice to see
life is happening perfectly,
life is a joyous experience, and
life is bright like the Crimson Light.

I am now open and receptive to the guidance of the Crimson Light;
therefore, I am trusting the choice I have made to
accept help,
embrace support, and
bless everything and everyone.

The words of my mouth,
The meditation of my heart,
The works of my hands,
And the steps of my feet had been accepted.
It was in the spirit of oneness.
A joy so immense and unfathomable,
How can one ever describe it to another?
Who has not yet begun to even dream?

CHAPTER 8

I Know Why I am Here

The elders stepped back and formed a wide circle as I looked up to the heavens, and there were sparkling bright lights all around. It was the Crimson Light, but this time, even brighter than I had seen in GPS. I was moved to tears at the brilliant reception that all the heavens, including the elders, cried with me. For once, I was allowed to cry freely in the presence of others without guilt or fear. And I tasted the tears that had fallen from the heavens that merged with those of my own. It was evident that my endurance of frequent intervals of retreat into stillness and confusion had paid off. I was sensing everything at the right time, space, and sequence, as crystal light.

Having graduated to four levels, I saw that each elder had been granted an award each, in his chosen field of the Mastership Love Program: the gifts of Wisdom, Healing, Prophesy, Knowledge, Language, Faith, Miracles, and Discernment being the shared gift of harness.

The simplicity of this wonderful understanding had resonated so deep inside that it actually caused me to laugh so hilariously that the elders joined in. It felt so good that I was able to laugh freely because I knew that they understood what Christ had said: Cry with those who cry and laugh with those who laugh, for that is how we win friends and influence others. We also demonstrate our willingness to allow them to be. Then there followed crackling sounds of lightning from the heavens, and once more, the evidence of oneness was conveyed.

The laughing had stopped, and the echo thinned away into nothingness, until there was stillness. Then I birthed an unacceptable "Aha" exclamation at my realisation that I was actually in the Mastership Love Programme. The elders acknowledged my awareness of the fact that they had indeed been training me. My cheeks felt as though they were holding up the whole world, as I smiled with delight. But the notion to rest evolved into a laugh that caused me to cackle louder than I ever did before, and it ended when I suddenly sneezed. Then there came the brightest lightning that I had ever seen. By that, I understood that lightning was only frightening because it shined on everything, even when we see what lies way within the soul.

Through my sense of wholeness, I shouted with joy, and it thundered until I had to breathe in deeply and exhale fully, once more. Then a gust of wind followed and caused us to sway. As we were moving from left to right, I remembered the beautiful cornfield with blooming heads. In that moment, all my ecstasies synthesised as Presence. And then, I wept, ceaselessly and more than I ever did before, even with Spenks. Nevertheless, this time I wept for joy because I was experiencing the most beautiful moment of my life.

As I wept a second time, there followed a downpour of heavy rain that stopped each time I stopped weeping. I became aware that the heavens were responding perfectly to my will. So just for the fun of it, I expanded the universe with the breath of my mouth, and I shifted the sounds and intonations of my voice, as I exclaimed, "I was lost but now I'm found."

I also referenced the fact that I had truly been favoured with the gift of a wide enough mouth that echoed to the universe and returned back to me. Then, I realised how Mother had indeed blessed me to find my voice. Sacrificing the expression of her own voice was the need to exhibit the flip side of the coin. Consequently, I had been initiated as the voice of not only those who had gone with the passing of their last breath but other people who had been (and still are) at risk of being abused.

As I shouted even louder, there was a tremor that confirmed the end of the incubation of my words: "Prepare to hear the tumbling sounds, because all Jericho walls must come down!"

The revelation that Wisdom consists of all the other elders, and Love consists of Wisdom, was a call for celebration on more than one level. I was on the Bridge of Actualising Self-full Love; I was with the elders who had guided me; I was also with Love; and evidently, I had Endurance to know why I was there. The spirit of Unity had blissfully bonded all of these factors into my consciousness, by which I was able to see Love. This time, I had no need to seek Forgiveness. The price had already been paid for what I was about to do. Now, since I certainly had no need to hide, I danced with Faith and Conviction, like I had never danced before. I knew that my steps would not sway, and so I also danced with Truth to express my enchantment with Endurance, and everywhere we turned, of course, there was Presence.

> Then another light breeze blew across the bridge,
> And the trees were dancing with such ease.
> Whilst they synchronised so beautifully
> Along with our swaying arms.
> My eyes beheld the shades of the blue sky
> And the shifting of white clouds,
> And then, I felt even more alive.

They'd formed circles and intersections of circles, including the shadows below that reflected their multiplicity. Heaven had merged with earth, and earth had merged with heaven. As though the broken circles had come together and had formed whole figures of eights (8), sideways, showed the symbol of infinity. By that, I also saw if you were to position two Cs, like Fear's weakest link, facing each other, it would also form the figure 8. For this reason, it's imperative that you stand face to face with Fear and have Faith to overcome any obstacle in your endeavours. Fear's weakest link becomes your strongest: infinitely whole, standing like the figure eight, and ultimately consisting of all elements of heaven and earth. Remember: Once in that position, you are no longer broken or the weakest link.

Besides the eights (8s), there was an overlap of opposing "Cs" that gave the impression that they had been super-imposed to form "Os" whole. On close examination, I saw that I had actually gone round in circles, but also at varying levels. I had walked the path that formed a semicircle outside the schoolyard, the template by which I had walked alongside the woman in black. That, in turn, seemed to seek its counterpart, and right into the basement of GPS. In essence, it was a spiral stairway that, when unfold and fully expanded, formed an "O."

There was my fine-tuned summary: I had spiralled down the basement of the figure eight. By that, I was able to examine the seat of my soul and heal my life, through the movement of the Crimson Light.

Hence, I demonstrated my own acts with Faith to attain my wish to be whole on the Bridge of Actualising Self-full Love. I cannot tell how exactly and at what stages my life changed but for sure, tremendous change occurred. It is perhaps safe to say chnge happened at the moment of my decision, the seed for growth was planted. It was at this point I was presented the opportunity to step up to the mark or back out of the game, so to speak; and to ensure my acknowledgement of being with Prese nce and having Conviction

Now I am experiencing wholeness on the Bridge of Actualising Self-full Love, whilst taking my rides through heaven and earth, by which I discovered the power of coincidences in my life.

> Call it what you wish: Manipulation or Godi-pulation,
> But that's what I understand true SynchroDestiny to be:
> That the constant illumination of the Crimson Light
> Had shined on me through my darkest night.

I had been healed from the generational curse of separateness that had resulted as a broken part of the wholeness of life's course. I also understood that being off course is the curse that one must be willing to accept. It also is the curse before you can get back on course of wholeness (O). Hence, it was prophesied that to get on the Bridge of Actualising Self-full Love, you must be born again. There, you can take your wings up to the heavens, a butterfly from which, before then, you must crawl in order to find your cure by going through your own metamorphosis. The illusion: "I cannot" becomes no more, for as in the same way cells of the body rush to protect a wound, likewise, you will be protected by the elders.

I had merged with the seven elders, which comprise the seven Pillars of Wisdom, to become a specialist of my own gift. I prayed that Love would continue to expand his kingdom, thus demonstrating my sense of wholeness. Now since everything is entailed in this wholeness, I was able to see a universal size whole that had comprised various "Cs," forming 8s upon 8s and looking like the petals, of the crown of thorns. Consequently, representing the cake that we must partake of life's pains in order to find our gains, simply because we are all part of the whole. Now, I not only consist of the essence of all the elders, but I am also infinite Love.

When the circle is broken, where life conditions are experienced as thorns, we can always choose one of the features of the Holy Trinity, by attending GPS, where you can undergo a health check, or finding your healing in HFTP, or stepping into your own smoky black hole of the Final Destination Resort, as Mr Barack Altidore did. These avenues you choose will show nothing is ever final, nor to be feared, as your new thoughts and actions align themselves accordingly to achieving your goals. That is to say, one can always find something familiar in himself which he can to attach to, in order to achieve his desire, and that, my dear, is the chameleon dance, choreographed by the Crimson Light.

Once in a circle, who can fail, for is this not where Unity lies, in synchronising all the elements of your dance?

However, I must admit, if it had not been for Oprah Winfrey, who spoke my language and empathised with my life experiences on her TV show, I believe I would still be part of the broken circle: a curse, still on course, looking for a cure. All this, I was led to do through the teachings of the woman in black, raising consciousness, by demonstrating that we are more alike than different. Such sweetness is like marrow to the bone, that not only increases in acceptance of oneself, but also the other, thereby making language an art that decorates the hearts of individuals, nations, and kingdoms, but one privy to many with discretion, through Oprah's gift as spirited language.

Like a child with my long-wished doll named Wilma, and with no inhibitions, I felt in flow to make my own show.

"Pardon me, Love, but I just want to say I am in awe of your magnificence, the way you sway to perfection life's chameleon dance in my reflection, and even through many challenges of uncertainties, you still make it a wonderful and heavenly romance on the Bridge of Actualising Self-full Love." Furthermore, what else could I have said? I simply fell to my knees, and instantly, in that moment, I began to sing like I had never sung before: a conscious halleluiah, for each corner of the earth: "Halleluiah, Halleluiah, Halleluiah, Halleluuuuuuuuiah," and all the elders joined in, till the heavens were filled with joy, and its tear drops fell, and there was oneness.

Though individually spirited, each elder had substituted the flip side of his own gift, but in essence, they worked as one spirit. I saw that without Fear, I would not have been with Faith, to declare myself free of guilty charges and to enjoy the richness of Iyanla's gift as spirited Faith. This, in turn, allowed me to learn how to pardon not only others but also myself, with Resignation, by which I inherited the master-key to Forgiveness. Although countless times, I struggled to find her use, amazingly, all I needed was the willingness to accept. Oh, what goodness, that wonderful day when my son came to me with a book and said, "This one is not written by Susan Jeffers, but I think you will like her anyway. In fact, that's what the man at the shop said." This was how I discovered that I could heal my life through the gift as Spirited Healing, with Louise Hay.

However, it was through Conviction that I knew I had truly been forgiven, and under a different guise, I had referred to him as Dirty Harry. It saddened me, the way he just unlocked the tombed casket without as much as a peep or a word. I had not appreciated the power of unspoken words. Now, I am eternally grateful for having Conviction, through the primary guise of Dejhuty, who performed a miracle that unlocked my womb. Now I know, like Mr Altidore, I will be with Conviction when I'll be ready for my own tomb. In the meantime, I'll be certain to continue to take Moringa, in order to lengthen my days on this plane. I extend my gratitude for Dejhuty's gift as spirited miracles.

And it was the loyalty of my friend Chatterbox that showed how to flip sides with Presence everywhere. Encapsulating the air of all beauty and all of life's singing and swinging through Maya's gift as spirited Wisdom. That was how I was able to 'rise' and to be conceive with Endurance through Love, for where there is Wisdom, there is Love.

You see, the Crimson Light never ceases to offer us chances.

Finally, I was able to draw on our parallels of events, though often perceived as madness, but they would prove the ultimate sanity:

Mr Barack Altidore descended into the smoky tombed casket, just like that, and under the guise of Denzel's performance, combatted the commands of a microchip in his head; both mirrored my own experiences as being on edge yet evidently transformed as Endurance.

Love, I feel the captivation of Presence forever with me through Maya's virtue of kindness and tenderness, as I bear witness to your tremendous grace in all of creation, thus touching even the toughest of souls.

Love, so patient and so kindly, gave me a nod, as though beckoning me to continue. Wow, I was actually being listened to because I had been accepted. I must say that I am thankful that Endurance overcame the power of the mental intrusion of Meryl Streep's insertion of a microscopic chip in his head, just so Liev Schreiber could rule in The Manchurian Candidate. Even in that dance, it seemed like you, Love, were just showing the other side of the coin, that you are not a part, but indeed, you are whole.

Denzel had taken on the role to show the whole world what had been prophesied had to manifest: that with Endurance, one can be made whole. That is, once you find something like a link in yourself in which to attach to Endurance. The only thing Endurance had mentioned is how deep I had to go to find that something like himself in me, to which I could attach myself. Perhaps Endurance had not bothered to find out how deep I had pushed down that something inside me. Then again, it might have been the very purpose of the gift, that I was able to see the hole in which Mr Altidore had stepped in, just like that.

Despite the pain of shedding and dying of self into the ground for becoming a star, it is through that process I gained the understanding that anyone can be a star. As long as you shine your light, you are a star. However, it's important to remember, you only need to get ignite to shine your light. Being a star is a requirement of your soul that seeks permission which is solely granted by you to illuminate,.

Like Denzel's gift as spirited prophecy to deliver the execution, I would be tried as silver tried in a furnace of earth, purified seven times. Now I understand that the elders had also been through their furnace, and that stands to reason why the true significance of silver is indeed infinite.

Now this is where the true essence of my soul's transformation lies; it is the question that I have not addressed before: How could it be, without the "C" as the weakest link, that I would find the valve inside that would ignite the spark of the Crimson Light in me? How else would the Crimson Light ultimately burn way down deep in my soul, thus forming and creating a Bridge to Actualising Self-full Love, by which I would be surrounded by the elders? All this happened because it was clear, at least in my head, that the diary of my choice, although it was not there in GPS, that did not mean one does not exist elsewhere. It was on this reflection I understood that clear thinking begat clear answers, because they both lie in the head.

I had made a conscious choice not to settle for second best, because I was no longer in Mrs Promise's class, so why should I settle for a C? Though, in effect, I would not disregard its significance to not only let me see but also extract more of what was birthing me.

I could have settled for anything like that lovely cornfield, swaying with blooming heads. However, I have now found a far greater treasure: packaged in vibrant shades of yellow, orange, and red, with seven gifts inside, each wrapped in Love and to make my specific choice. All this, I must say, has by far exceeded any expectation for the replacement of the two-page written diary. I have now found another that would prove to the world that there truly exists a record of my personal life transformation: a true confirmation of the magic of Crimson Light.

Now if you were to ask me, "Why are you here?" the answer would be clear: I know why I am here. I am here to share with you my insights of the magic of the Crimson Light and my exhilarating experience of being on the Bridge of Actualising Self-full Love. I now permit you to not only read my diary, but to also feel free to underline its passages. Hence, I dedicate the essence of this life transformational journey, as my wish for you, with Love.

Such a blessing! For what greater love has a man than to literally step into a tombed casket, just like that? I found the courage to not only witness, but also learn how to lay all down, for I am the mother of many sons. I now savour this perfect bliss on the Bridge of Actualising Self-full Love.

To Mr Barack Altidore, for the inspiration and blessing of the vision, I really could not ignore, even though I had no idea that I would have Endurance to complete my journey through the black smoky hole that saved my soul. For this reason, I remain eternally grateful, as a graduate of the Open University of Life, sponsored by Love, through the Crimson Light.

There are no accidents and no coincidences, but the choices that we make.

Useful Information before Boarding

Some useful information before making your journey to the Bridge of Actualising Self-full Love:

Tickets are available through all outlets, to be found in your life's experiences.

Your commitment will determine the cost, which is refundable.

However, you are required to just trust that you will not encounter any hidden cost. It's a fair game.

There is always the luxury of a bursary to ensure your place on the Bridge of Actualising Self-full Love.

Remember, life is a cycle, and so is the Bridge of Actualising Self-full Love: It moves in circles.

You can hop on at any time, any minute or second of any day.

There is always the choice to hop off at any time, but first, ask yourself, do you really want to waste the precious gift of time?

The journey will be at your pace; the elders will take care of you.

The only cost is the prerequisite to let go of pride, guilt, and shame. They only serve as clothing of distortion.

You never have to worry about the carrier's capacity, because you must be light. Just get on board.

You may have to say goodbye to your friends and family. Just say that you are going on a vacation, and that's no lie, since you are certain to have the time of your life on the bridge anyway.

Be warned! Your friends and family may not recognise you on your return, as they will be profoundly enchanted with the glow all around you, from head to toe.

This, however, will not only serve as a confirmation that you have travelled, but that you are now expressing your ability to confidently walk your talk.

Furthermore, you really won't care, anyway, if the whole world knows and notices the new label, "Divine Acceptance," specifically designed by the Crimson Light.

Please note: This is not a one-size-fits-all but is exclusively tailored for a perfect fit for each individual perfectly through the journey onto the Bridge of Actualising Self-full Love.

Attention, all!

This is an announcement from the Crimson Light!
We are happy to inform you
Your bridge 747 (seven four seven) is ready and waiting.
Therefore, please get your boarding pass ready
For your journey of a lifetime
Onto the Bridge of Actualising Self-full Love.